The Flying Cat

And Other Amazing Stories of the
Washington Monument
Jim Berard

*Foreword by **Edwin C. Bearss**,*
Historian Emeritus, National Park Service

D1312254

Capitol Books of Maryland
Arnold, Maryland

Second Edition published by
Capitol Books of Maryland
573 Kevins Drive
Arnold, MD 21012

Original Edition published by
EPM Publications, Inc.
Delaplane, VA

Book Design by
Tom Huestis
John Corpus
Tom Gnidovic

Library of Congress Cataloging-in-Publication Data

Berard ,Jim, 1952-
    The flying cat and other amazing stories of the Washington Monument / Jim Berard ;
foreword by Edwin C. Bearrs.

    p. cm.
    Includes bibliographical references.
    ISBN 1-889324-20-5

    Second Edition ISBN 0-9786462-0-7

    1. Washington Monument (Washington, D.C.)--History--Anecdotes. 2. Washington
Monument (Washington, D.C.)--Miscellanea. 3. Washinton (D.C.)--Buildings, structures,
etc--Anecdotes. 4. Washington (D.C.)--Buildings, structures, etc--Miscellanea. I. Title:
Flying cat. II. Title

F203.4.W3 B47 2000
975.3--dc21
                                                                          00-037121

Contents

The Washington Monument today.

From the Author

The Washington Monument—or, as my nephew, Jimmy, used to call it, the "Tall Skinny Thing"—is the most visible and recognizable landmark in our Nation's Capital. Constructed in the ancient Egyptian design of an obelisk and standing over 555 feet tall, the monument once reigned as the tallest manmade object in the world. Today it has lost that distinction to modern iron and steel towers. However, Washington's monument still retains the title of tallest free-standing stone building in the world.

Each year, some 800,000 visitors from around the world take the 70-second elevator ride to the monument's observation deck, 500 feet above Washington, D.C. They marvel at the unobstructed views of the White House, the U.S. Capitol, the Tidal Basin, the Lincoln and Jefferson Memorials and other familiar sights of the capital city. Few of these visitors, however, know the long, glorious, and sometimes tortured history of Washington's monument. Fewer know of the 194 stones, many with exotic histories of their own, that line the walls of the monument's interior staircase. Fewer still have heard the fascinating stories of heroism, intrigue, showmanship, and human interest that have been associated with the structure since the colonial Congress first conceived of a monument to George Washington in 1783.

The purpose of this book is to share this history, these hidden treasures, and these fascinating tales of the Washington Monument with everyone who has an interest in learning more about this stately tower of stone, the centerpiece of the National Mall and the nation's tall, skinny, but majestic, tribute to the Father of Our Country.

I would like to thank Rangers Jim Lance and Donnie Smith, who helped me in my early days as a Park Service volunteer.

And a special thanks to the incomparable Ed Bearss for his participation in this project.

Foreword

No monument here and few abroad are better known or command the awe that is accorded the Washington Monument. Long before my first visit to the nation's capital in late March, 1938, during spring vacation while a student at St. John's Military Academy at Delafield, Wis., I was familiar with the monument. With other members of the group, I ascended the towering structure to the viewing deck by the elevator, and, with the adventurous, descended the 898-step staircase. In doing so, my friends and I noted the memorial stones, and if a home state had one, it was a source of pride, if not of disappointment.

I came to know the Washington Monument better in the future. In the autumn of 1946, after four years' service in the U.S. Marine Corps, I returned to Washington to attend the Georgetown University School of Foreign Service under the GI Bill. During the next three springs and summers, I got to know the Washington Monument as player-manager of a softball team which participated in a Sunday morning league that played on the monument grounds. There were a number of walks down the monument stairway and at least one struggle up.

As heretofore the stones continued to intrigue me. Then, there were the stories about the structure, its construction, and associated history told by long-time residents, some based on fact, others on folklore. At least one of these, the one highlighting the catch of a baseball thrown from the observation deck by Preston Gibson and caught by Charles "Gabby" Street, I was long cognizant of, having heard of it during my grade school years in Montana from my father, a die-hard baseball fan.

Now, thanks to Jim Berard, as the second millennium ends, visitors to the structure, be they veterans or first-timers, as well as those who savor good history, can learn about the Washington Monument. The construction history, the associated controversies, the stories behind memorial stones, and the monument and its trials and tribulations are told in a fast-moving and graceful style underscoring Berard's credentials as an historian and journalist. Better yet, he writes with an enthusiasm for his subject that underscores his dedication and love of the monument, its significance, and his willingness to share his knowledge. Master storyteller Berard weaves diverse threads of the monument's story into a fine tapestry titled *The Flying Cat and Other Amazing Stories of the Washington Monument.* This publication will enrich a visit to the grand monument to the father of our country, fittingly eulogized by Light Horse Harry Lee as, "first in war, first in peace, first in the hearts of his countrymen."

Edwin C. Bearss
Historian Emeritus
National Park Service

WASHINGTON NATIONAL MONUMENT

Robert Mills' original design for the Washington Monument.

Chapter One

The 101-Year Construction Project

The idea for a monument to our First President came well before George Washington held that office. A monument was ordered by the Congress of the Confederation as a tribute to General, not President, Washington. It took another 65 years for construction to begin on the monument, and 36 more before the monument's completion. In the meantime, the concept of a national monument to George Washington took many different shapes.

A Man on a Horse

In 1783, in the final days of the American Revolution, Congress, meeting in Princeton, N.J., under the Articles of Confederation, called for the erection of a statue to Washington in the federal capital. Even though no one voting on that resolution knew where the permanent capital would be, the Congress had very detailed specifications for the Washington tribute.

The monument, as then envisioned, would be a statue of General Washington mounted on horse. The statue's pedestal would bear the names of major events in the War for Independence.

Congress' inability to decide where to locate the national capital prevented the order for the equestrian statue from being executed. In 1787, the Constitutional Convention assembled in Philadelphia to resolve problems the states experienced in dealing with each other and the federal government under the Articles of Confederation. Presided over by General Washington, the convention did more than revamp the Articles. It created an entirely new framework for the government: the Constitution of the United States of America.

When the Constitution was ratified by the 13 states and Washington was elected the first President, Congress selected a site straddling the Potomac River in Maryland and Virginia for a permanent home for the federal government. A French architect named Pierre L'Enfant was hired to design the new capital city, and L'Enfant included a site for the monument to Washington at a point very close to where the Washington Monument stands today. L'Enfant did not envision the 55-story stone tower now on the site, however. He was still thinking about a man on a horse.

The Empty Tomb

There was little progress on the monument project until President Washington died in 1799. Shortly after his death, a motion was introduced in Congress to renew the effort to erect a monument to the Father of our Country. The resolution, however, changed the project from one of an outdoor statue to a mausoleum for Washington's remains to be built inside the Capitol building, which was under construction at the time. The House and Senate approved the resolution, but, due to more pressing business, no further action was taken on this proposal.

A year later, Rep. Henry Lee of Virginia, a friend of Washington's, revived the equestrian monument proposal. Lee's resolution was amended, however, and the design of the monument was changed to a mausoleum to be built on the Capitol grounds.

Architect Benjamin Henry Latrobe was consulted. Latrobe designed much of the Capitol and was noted for his expertise in the Greek Revival style.

Latrobe recommended a pyramid, 100 feet square at the base, featuring 19 steps to the top, and decorated with appropriate Greek Revival ornamentation. Congress approved the design, but appropriated no construction funds, so nothing was done.

In 1816, the State of Virginia sought to have Washington's remains relocated to Richmond, the state's capital. This prompted a second Congressional resolution calling for the construction of a tomb for Washington in the Capitol building itself. The architect of the Capitol incorporated Congress' resolution into the building's design and included a tomb for George and Martha Washington directly beneath the dome in the lower crypt. After much negotiation, however, Washington's heirs bowed to the General's wishes, as written in his will, that his final resting place be on the grounds of his estate at Mount Vernon, Virginia, eight miles south of the capital city. A third attempt to bring Washington's body to the city that bears his name was led by Sen. Henry Clay of Kentucky in 1832, but Washington's family would not yield, and his body remains at Mount Vernon, in a mausoleum Washington himself designed.

Today the tomb in the Capitol stands empty… For many years it housed the Lincoln Catafalque, a wooden funeral platform draped in black velvet, originally used to hold the casket of President Abraham Lincoln when the assassinated President lay in state in the Capitol Rotunda in 1865. The catagalque has been used for dignitaries who have lain in state since then, including Predidents, Members of Congress, and the warriors en route to the Tomb oth the Unkonwns in Arlington National Cemetery. The catafalque was moved to the new Capitol Visitor Center in 2008.

Bury Me at Mount Vernon

"The family Vault at Mount Vernon requiring repairs, and being improperly situated besides, I desire that a new one of Brick, and upon a larger Scale, may be built at the foot of what is commonly called the Vineyard Inclosure,—on the ground which is marked out—In which my remains, with those of my deceased relatives (now in the old Vault) and such others of my family as may chuse to be entombed there, may be deposited.—And it is my express desire that my Corpse may be Interred in a private manner, without—parade, or funeral Oration."

—*from the last will and testament of George Washington*

Washington as Zeus

With efforts to move Washington's body to the capital foundering, Congress turned to a fourth concept for a monument to the hero of the Revolution and the first President. In 1830 Congress commissioned a marble statue of Washington by sculptor Horatio Greenough to be placed in the rotunda of the Capitol.

Greenough based his creation on the heroic statue of the Greek god Zeus at the Temple at Olympia, one of the Seven Wonders of the Ancient World. The completed work was placed in the Capitol in 1841. The statue showed Washington seated, stripped to the waist, wearing a toga, sandals, and a crown of laurels. Despite the classic heritage of this work, many Americans of the day could not accept a monument depicting a half-naked, imperial Washington. Critics enjoyed poking fun at the statue. One wit observed the statue made the first President look as if he had just stepped out of the bath. Another imagined Washington to be saying, "Give me liberty or give me death, but for God's sake give me some clothes!"

The work was eventually removed from the Capitol, and now resides in the Smithsonian Institution's Museum of American History.

During the same session, Congress also commissioned a more traditional—and acceptable—tribute to Washington: a full-length portrait by New York artist John Vanderlin. That portrait now hangs in the House of Representatives chamber, to the left of the Speaker's chair. Across the room, to the right of the Speaker, is a portrait of the Marquis de Lafayette, Washington's friend and ally in the War for Independence.

Getting Serious:
The Washington National Monument Society

By 1833, with Congressional interest waning in any further tributes to Washington, George Watterston, a city alderman and former Librarian of Congress, decided the time had come to move the monument idea forward. Watterston, along with a group of other prominent Washingtonians, called a public meeting in September of that year, and the Washington National Monument Society was formed for the sole purpose of building a national monument to President Washington. The project was to be paid for by private contributions, bypassing the Congressional appropriations process.

Chief Justice of the United States John Marshall was elected the society's first president. When Marshall died two years later, the post was offered to former President James Madison, but under Madison the office became mostly ceremonial. Following Madison's death in

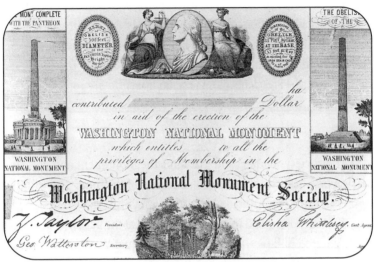

The Washington National Monument Society presented certificates such as this one (c. 1850) to people who contributed money to the Washington Monument project. Note that the certificate depicts both Robert Mills' original design for the monument, which included a statuary hall or "pantheon" at the base, and the obelisk alone. At the time, construction was underway on the obelisk, but the society still held out the possibility of adding the pantheon if it could come up with the money.

1836, the society decided to bestow the honorary position on the President of the United States, ex officio.

Vocabulary Lesson: Ex Officio

Ex officio means "by virtue of an official position." It is Latin for "from office." In other words, the President of the United States, just because he holds that office, gets to head the Washington National Monument Society. Therefore, the President holds the additional position ex officio.

The society made grand plans for the monument and solicited design proposals from the noted architects of the time. The winning proposal came from Robert Mills of South Carolina, who designed a square stone tower, 600 feet tall, surrounded at the base by a 100-foot-high pillared hall of statues honoring not just Washington, but all Presidents. (If today's Washington Monument were placed on top of the Jefferson Memorial, it would look a little like Mills' original plan.)

The monument society had grand plans, but the collection of funds to pay for the project lagged considerably behind. The society began to question if it could afford Mills' design. Congress even got into the act. In 1844, the House Committee on Public Buildings and Grounds, in providing a site for the monument, developed its own design. The committee recommended that the monument take the form of a domed temple with a statue of Washington atop the dome. It recommended further that the building should have sufficient room for statues and artwork honoring all Presidents. Thanks to opposition from the society, Congress defeated this proposal.

Finally, in 1848, Congress approved a site on the National Mall, directly west of the Capitol and south of the White House, very near the place identified for the equestrian statue of Washington in L'Enfant's original plan for the capital city. The monument could not be built on the exact spot selected by L'Enfant, however, because the ground there was not stable enough to support the massive tower. A more suitable building site just to the south and east of L'Enfant's designated spot was chosen for the monument.

That same year, the monument society determined it had enough money to begin construction. However, the society also scaled back Mills' design and decided to build only the stone obelisk, not the statuary hall at its base. Although the society left the question of the statuary hall open in case funds became available for adding it to the project, that part of Mills' design was never built.

Vocabulary Lesson:
Obelisk and Cenotaph

The Washington Monument is an obelisk. As defined by Webster's New World Dictionary, an obelisk is "a tall, four-sided pillar tapering to a pyramidal top." It comes from the Greek word obelos which means "needle."

Obelisks were commonly used in ancient Egypt to honor pharaohs and queens. They were usually carved from a solid block of stone. The Washington Monument is the largest obelisk in the world, but it is made up of 36,000 stones and has a hollow center where the stairway and elevator shaft are located.

The monument is also a cenotaph, which Webster defines as "a monument honoring a dead person whose body is somewhere else." It comes from the Greek words keno ("empty') and taphos ("tomb").

In the course of this book, you will see the word "obelisk" used several more times. This, however, will be the last time you will have to read the word "cenotaph."

Breaking Ground

With great pomp and ceremony, on July 4, 1848, the cornerstone of the Washington Monument was laid. President James K. Polk attended. Speaker of the House Robert C. Winthrop gave the keynote address, and spoke for an hour and a half. A crowd of some 20,000 witnessed the event.

The Washington Monument in its early stages of construction.

Dignitaries included Dolley Madison, widow of the President, and Mrs. Alexander Hamilton. Also in attendance were Martha Washington's grandson, George Washington Parke Custis, and a first-term Congressman from Illinois, Rep. Abraham Lincoln.

The cornerstone weighed 24,500 pounds and contained a zinc box in which were placed, among other things, plans for the monument, a bible, coins, newspapers of the day, and copies of the U.S. Constitution and Declaration of Independence. The cornerstone was laid in a Masonic ceremony officiated by the Grand Master of the capital city's Masonic Lodge, wearing the very same sash and apron as President Washington wore at the ceremony laying the cornerstone for the Capitol 55 years earlier.

Following the ceremony, work progressed quickly. The stone tower reached a height of 126 feet by the end of 1852. However, contributions were still not coming in quickly enough for the project to keep pace. The society had to scrap its $1.00 limit on donations in order to collect more revenue. It also scaled back Mills' plan even further, limiting the obelisk's height to 500 feet, instead of the 600-foot tower Mills envisioned.

Then, in 1854, things got really bad.

Where Did You Say They Put It?

In 1948, preparations were made to commemorate the 100th anniversary of the laying of the Washington Monument's cornerstone. The Masonic Lodge brought out the apron and sash used at the original ceremony. Documents were researched and speeches were reviewed. Everything was ready, except no one knew where the cornerstone was.

Records and news accounts of the original ceremony were sketchy, but indicated that the stone was laid at the northeast corner of the building. Further research showed that the cornerstone was most likely placed in the foundation of the monument, not in the shaft. It is also likely that the stone was covered by later additions to the foundation. ⟶

Sixteen blocks east of the monument, a similar puzzle faced the Architect of the Capitol when he tried to locate that building's cornerstone for its bicentennial in 1993. Accounts of that ceremony indicate the stone was laid in the building's southeast corner. The question was which southeast corner?

The Capitol was built in sections. The north (Senate) wing was built first, then the south (House) wing. The building's center section, containing the dome and rotunda as well as the tomb designed for George Washington, was built last. Traditionally, it was assumed that the ceremony took place at the southeast corner of the first section to be built, the north wing. For many years, a plaque on the wall outside the old Supreme Court chamber on the building's first floor indicated that the stone was in the wall behind it.

When the Architect's office tried to verify the location, however, it could not locate such a stone. The investigation then shifted to the south wing of the building. There, under the Capitol coffee shop, the Architect found a stone in the foundation that he believed to be the missing cornerstone.

(The architect made this determination by the size of the stone. It was much larger than the stones around it, too large to be just another construction block. It was not yet the custom in 1793 to engrave any special markings on the stone, so the architect could not use such markings to identify the cornerstone.)

Instead of erecting a bronze plaque the Architect chose not to mark the stone's location. Today, the excavation site has been repaired and repainted with no indication of the historic find below.

Adding further to the puzzle, however, was the lack of silver traces in the fill dirt surrounding the foundation. Reports of the day said that when the Capitol's cornerstone was put in place, it was laid on top of an engraved silver plate. Searching for the stone 200 years later, the Architect thought that the plate would have left silver traces

→

in the soil as it decayed over the years and those traces would lead to the cornerstone. The stone found in the south wing's foundation is most likely the cornerstone, but there were no silver traces present. No one knows what happened to the silver plate on which the stone was set.

Let Us Interrupt You:
The Know Nothings Bankrupt the Project

In 1853 and 1854, politics and bigotry combined to put a temporary end to the construction of the Washington Monument. A political faction called the "Know Nothings", angered over the acceptance of a memorial stone from Pope Pius IX, nearly shut the project down for good. On March 14, 1854, a group of Know Nothings outraged the nation by stealing the Pope's Stone and throwing it in the Potomac River. (Read more about the Know Nothings and the theft of the Pope's Stone in Chapter Three.)

Not content just to keep the Pope out of the monument, the Know Nothings also felt they could manage the project better than the current board of the Washington National Monument Society. On Washington's Birthday, February 22, 1854, the Know Nothings took control of the organization in a rigged election. It took three years to wrest control of the society from the Know Nothings. By that time, however, the private donations that were being collected to finance construction had dried up, buildings and equipment had fallen into disrepair, and the project was bankrupt.

Despite pleas to Congress, the struggle over slavery and the approach of the Civil War prevented any federal appropriations from coming forward, and the unfinished monument sat abandoned for two decades more.

Nativists and Know Nothings

A growing distrust of immigrants, particularly Roman Catholic immigrants, took root in many parts of America during the mid-19th Century. This distrust grew into a political movement known as "Nativism." The Nativists, who were mostly native-born Protestants, believed that these Catholic immigrants posed a danger to America. They believed that the Pope would be able to exercise influence over the affairs of the United States if the immigrants were allowed to gain the right to vote and hold office. As the Catholic population grew, the Nativists believed, so would the Pope's power, blurring the separation of Church and State, potentially even ending religious freedom in the United States. This belief persisted among many Americans well into the 20th Century, and was even a factor in opposition to the 1960 election of John F. Kennedy, the first Catholic President of the United States.

By 1854, the Nativist movement had given birth to the American Party, or the Know Nothings. The party earned its nickname because of the secrecy of the organization. When asked about their party's affairs, members would simply dismiss the question by saying, "I know nothing about that."

In its time, the party achieved modest political success, electing governors and Congressmen in a handful of states and running ex-President Millard Fillmore as its candidate for the White House in 1856. Discredited by the raid on the Washington Monument and the takeover of the monument project, the party was soon overtaken by history. Slavery replaced immigration as the primary political issue in the country, and as the Civil War loomed, the American Party lost its political base. By 1861, the year President Lincoln took office and the Civil War began, the party had all but faded away.

The Man on the Horse Returns

As progress on Mills' obelisk slowed to a halt, Congress returned to its original plan of a statue of Washington mounted on a horse. In 1853, Congress passed a resolution to proceed with an equestrian statue to George Washington, as the Continental Congress had resolved 70 years earlier. An appropriation of $53,000 was approved for the project and the commission for the work went to sculptor Clark Mills.

In 1860, the statue was placed in Washington Circle, at the intersection of Pennsylvania Avenue, New Hampshire Avenue, K Street and 23rd Street NW in Washington, D.C., where it stands today.

In the meantime, the stone tower stood forlorn and abandoned, and would remain that way for another 20 years.

Where Soldiers Drilled and Cattle Grazed

The Washington Monument grounds today are popular with tourists enjoying the sights of Washington, and by locals using the open space to picnic, play team sports, sunbathe, bike, hear a concert or fly a kite. The grounds are open, well maintained, and welcoming to visitors.

During the Civil War years (1861-1865), though, the grounds were less inviting. The unfinished monument stood like a 15-story stone stump. Work had stopped three years before the war began, and the tower had only reached 156 feet. The flag of the Union flew from a mast affixed to its truncated top, as federal troops drilled on the grounds below. Nearby, pens held cattle waiting to be slaughtered to feed the Union regiments.

Across the Potomac River, Virginia had seceded from the Union to join the Confederacy, and would eventually host the Confederate capital. Union soldiers occupied Robert E. Lee's estate at Arlington, well within view of the monument grounds, and prepared to defend Washington, D.C., from a possible attack by General Lee and his Confederate army.

After the war, reconstruction of the South, the assassination of President Lincoln and the impeachment of President Andrew Johnson held the attention of the federal government. The Washington Monument stood incomplete on its hill overlooking the Potomac.

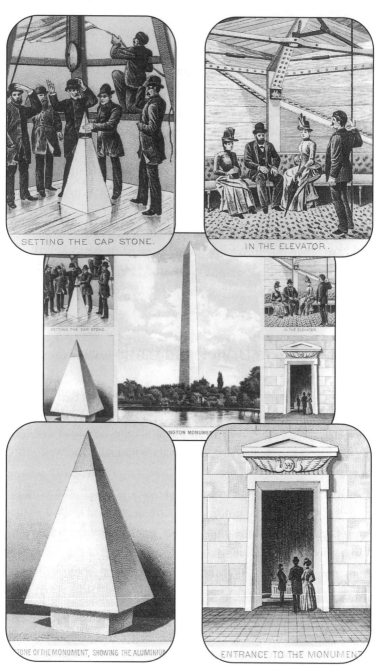

SETTING THE CAP STONE.

IN THE ELEVATOR.

STONE OF THE MONUMENT, SHOWING THE ALUMINIUM

ENTRANCE TO THE MONUMENT

A 19th century engraving presents a collection of images from the Washington Monument's early days, including the setting of the aluminum tip in 1884. The monument's entrance shown in the lower right picture was reduced and its ornamentation removed to give the monument's exterior a more uniform appearance.

Mark Twain described the unfinished obelisk as looking like "a factory chimney with the top broken off." George Alfred Townsend, correspondent for the *Chicago Tribune*, called the abandoned monument "a mournful instance of the short life of public impulse."

It was a national eyesore, not the majestic monument envisioned to glorify the memory of the first American President. The federal government had to make a decision: either finish the monument or tear it down.

Why Does the Monument Change Color?

Visitors to the Washington Monument often ask why the stone walls of the tower change color about 150 feet above the ground. Rangers and volunteers sometimes respond by joking that the last time the Park Service washed the walls, the ladder only reached that high, or that the change is due to a high-water mark left by a disastrous flood in the late 1800s. Sometimes the questioner even believes those far-fetched explanations.

Many visitors, and even some local tour guides, think that the color changes because construction of the monument was interrupted by the Civil War. That is only partially correct. A break in construction is the reason, but the interruption occurred well before Confederate Gen. Pierre G. T. Beauregard fired on Fort Sumter to spark the Civil War.

Construction stopped because the project had run out of money. Collections were falling woefully short of expenses by 1854, and the project suffered from four succeeding years of mismanagement by the Know Nothings. By the time control of the monument project was wrested from the hands of the Know Nothings, the coffers were empty. It can be correctly argued that the Civil War delayed resumption of the project, but the war was not the reason that construction had ceased.

When the work resumed in 1880, the monument's engineers tried to match the color of the existing marble as

⟶

closely as possible. The original stone had come from a quarry outside Baltimore, but the stratum, or layer, of marble from which it was extracted had been depleted. New stone had to be quarried from a deeper stratum and came out of the ground slightly darker than the marble already used in the monument's walls. After an unsuccessful attempt to match the color with stone from a New England quarry, the engineers decided to accept a slight but noticeable color difference and return to Maryland for the marble needed to complete the project.

Send in the Troops

The monument project found a champion in President Ulysses S. Grant, who lobbied Congress to provide the funding necessary to finish it. Finally, in 1876, Grant's last year in office, Congress appropriated $200,000 for the monument project. By agreement with the Monument Society, ownership of the monument and grounds would be turned over to the government.

A joint commission was created to supervise the completion of the project. The commission would consist of the President of the United States, the Supervising Architect of the Treasury Department, the Architect of the Capitol, the Chief Engineer of the U.S. Army, and the First Vice President of the Washington National Monument Society.

After two years of study and discussion, including talk of using the existing structure as the basis for a totally new design, the commission chose to stick with Mills' obelisk.

Lt. Col. Thomas Lincoln Casey was placed in charge of the project. Casey's first priority was to strengthen the monument's foundation. He had his men remove parts of the foundation that had deteriorated, and reinforce the remainder with concrete. Casey's men enlarged the foundation so that it went 13 feet deeper and covered two and a half times the area of the old foundation.

Casey's next task was removing the top six feet of the shaft. When the Know Nothings controlled the monument project in the 1850s, they used substandard stone, including scraps and rejects from earlier construction, in order to save money. The cheap construction and effects of weather during the 26-year interruption of the project caused many of the blocks above the 150-ft. level to crack and crumble, requiring their removal.

No Name Given

As applicants lined up for jobs at the monument site in 1878, the name on one application was listed as "No name given." Attached to the application was a brief letter to Chief Engineer Casey reading, "I will be gratified if you can give the bearer any employment on the work now being done on the monument grounds."

The note was written on stationery from the Columbia Institution for the Deaf and Dumb, and was signed by Dr. E. M. Gallaudet, the school's superintendent. The man would not give his name because he could not speak.

It is difficult to tell from existing records if the foreman hired the bearer of Gallaudet's note. If the man did get a job at the monument, it is likely that his employers would have determined his real name and used it on his work records. The link between any worker at the monument site and the applicant who could not give his name to the foreman is missing.

Today, the Columbia Institution for the Deaf and Dumb is known as Gallaudet University, and is one of the world's premier institutions of higher learning for the hearing- and speech-impaired.

A Perfect Obelisk

Casey made one more significant change to the monument. He altered Mills' design for the tower, changing the height to 555 feet, in order to make the monument a perfect obelisk. Casey based his decision on careful measurements of Egyptian obelisks by George Perkins Marsh, who was U.S. ambassador to Italy at the time. Marsh determined that a perfect obelisk was about 10 times as high as it was wide at its base. The unfinished Washington Monument was just over 55 feet square at its base, so it would have to reach a height of just over 550 feet to make it a perfect obelisk.

In 1880, the Washington Monument began to rise again. A second cornerstone was laid at the 150-ft. level by President Rutherford B. Hayes. On December 6, 1884, the marble capstone was set in place. The capstone was topped with an aluminum tip, set by Casey himself. A flag was unfurled from the top of the monument as cannons roared below. On that cold, blustery December day in 1884, 101 years after Congress first declared its intent to build a monument to General Washington, and 51 years after the formation of the Washington National Monument Society, the construction of the Washington Monument was completed.

Aluminum? As in Foil?

The choice of an aluminum tip for the monument strikes many people as odd. Today we would think of precious metals such as gold or platinum for the honor. However, in 1884, aluminum was a logical choice. At that time, aluminum was quite precious, at $1.10 per ounce. Casey also selected aluminum for its conductivity, in order to help protect the monument from lightning strikes. Also, aluminum does not rust or tarnish, and therefore would not stain the white marble beneath it.

The 100-ounce aluminum tip is a miniature pyramid, 5.6 inches square and 8.9 inches high. It was cast by William Frishmuth of Philadelphia. At the time, it was the largest block of aluminum ever cast, and earned a place in the window of Tiffany's, the famous New York jeweler.

Engraved on the aluminum tip were the names of the key people associated with the completion of the monument, significant dates in the monument's construction, and the declaration, "Laus Deo," ("Praise be to God"). Conspicuously absent from the names engraved on the tip were those of Robert Mills, the architect who proposed the original design, and George Watterston, who, in 1833, assembled the first meeting of what was to become the Washington National Monument Society.

A replica of the tip is on display inside the monument.

Going Up? Dedication and Early Operation

On February 21, 1885, the eve of the 153rd anniversary of George Washington's birth, the completed monument was dedicated with great pomp and pageantry. The ceremony included remarks by President Chester A. Arthur, who dedicated the structure to "the immortal name and memory of George Washington."

Although the monument was completed, it still wasn't ready for regular visitors. Decisions had to be made about the landscaping of the monument grounds. Casey proposed an ambitious terrace with underground entrances to the tower, but settled for a more modest plan to fill the area around the shaft with earth, creating a gently sloping hill that blends seamlessly into the rest of the National Mall.

Casey wanted the finished monument to present a clean, uniform look. So, he ordered the west entrance sealed and covered over with marble to match the exterior walls. He reduced the remaining east entrance from an ornamented 15-foot-high entry to a plain eight-foot opening. Casey added half-ton marble doors on bronze hinges and steel rollers that, when closed, blended with the monument's marble face. (The doors were later replaced by iron gates.)

The Corps of Engineers also had to refit the steam construction hoist, which was used to haul the stone blocks to the highest reaches of the monument, into an elevator suitable for passengers. The car was enclosed and safety devices were added.

Electric lights were added to illuminate the interior stairway. An improved lightning suppression system was installed. The remaining memorial stones were placed in the walls. (More on the memorial stones in Chapter Three.)

The monument opened to the public in October, 1888. The Joint Commission was dissolved and the Washington Monument was turned over to "the custody, care and protection of the Secretary of War."

Building a Better Monument: Improvements Continue

The construction of the monument and the finishing touches ended in 1888, but over the years more improvements were made.

In 1890, steam pipes were installed to bring heat to the ground floor. A waiting room with oak benches was added in 1904.

The old steam hoist was replaced with a modern electric elevator in 1900, and that elevator was replaced with newer models in 1926, 1959, and 2002.

New benches encircled the monument and trash cans were added at the base of the monument and to the grounds in 1963. Access for handicapped visitors improved in 1976 when a ramp was installed to make it easier for people in wheelchairs to reach the elevator.

Let There Be Lights!

The invention of the airplane brought more changes to the monument. The building's exterior was lit with powerful floodlights beginning in 1929. Red aircraft warning lights were placed in four of the monument 's eight windows in 1931. Pilots complained that the thick marble surrounding the windows limited the visibility of the lights. So, in 1958, eight holes were drilled above the windows and the current red, blinking clearance lights were installed. The exterior floodlights were also upgraded to illuminate the entire shaft.

The monument's floodlights were turned off during World War II to comply with blackout regulations. In January, 1945, a worker at the monument threw the wrong switch and the stone tower lit up in pre-war splendor. People who saw the lights go on thought the war had ended. Unfortunately, fighting continued for another four months in Europe and another seven months in the Pacific.

A Neon Monument?

One of the more novel ideas for illuminating the Washington Monument was submitted by Karl L. Gower, whose address was listed as the Central Y.M.C.A. in Washington, D.C.

In a letter to Rep. Jennings Randolph of West Virginia in 1936, Gower proposed lining the monument with red

→

Floodlights give the monument a dramatic look on Armistice Night, November 11, 1921.

neon lights. Gower said the red neon outline would make the monument more visible to passing aircraft, especially in rainy or foggy conditions. The glass tubing containing the neon gas would be nearly invisible when the lights were off during the day.

Gower recommended a similar treatment for the Capitol and Lincoln Memorial. Beyond the added protection from aircraft, Gower said the red outlines would give the buildings on the mall a distinctive, modern look.

Stars and Stripes Forever, 1922

February 22, 1922 (or 2/22/22, for those of you into numerology) brought a new addition to the Washington Monument when the tower was surrounded by a circle of 48 American flags—one for each state in the Union at the time—in observance of Washington's 190th birthday. The effect was very striking, and the ring of flags became a permanent feature of the monument.

In 1959, the configuration of the flags was changed to make room for two additions when Alaska and Hawaii gained statehood, and brought the total number of states, and flags, to 50. That same year, a bill proposed in the U.S. Senate would have flown a flag of the same design as when each state joined the union. The original 13 states, for example, would be represented by the flag with the familiar circle of 13 stars. Alaska, meanwhile, would have a 49-star flag flying for it. The bill went nowhere.

Another bill proposed four years later drew loud protests from the U.S. Army. A Congressman from California was appalled when he saw park rangers raising and lowering the flags around the monument without proper military ceremony. He introduced a bill giving the Army responsibility for raising and lowering the flags at the Washington Monument and other public monuments and memorials around the city.

The Army protested strongly, claiming it would require a detail of one officer, two noncommissioned officers, 100 enlisted men and a brass band just to raise the flags at the Washington Monument with proper military honors. It would require yet another 100 men to lower and properly fold the 50 flags at sunset. Although some Members of Congress sincerely doubted the Army's claim, the bill did not succeed.

A Refurbished Monument for the New Millennium

In 1996, the National Park Service undertook a four-year, $8 million restoration of theWashington Monument, the most extensive renovation in the building's history. Financed with a combination of public, private and corporate funds, the project included installing a new climate control system and new elevator machinery, and cleaning and repairing the 194 memorial stones lining the main stairway.

Most significantly, an aluminum scaffolding was erected to allow workers to repair and replace some 64,000 linear feet of exterior caulking, and inspect and repair the marble stones that make up the monument's exterior walls.

To give the scaffolding a more attractive appearance, architect Michael Graves designed a plan using blue mesh striping and special lighting to simulate the pattern and appearance of the monument's marble blocks. *(See photo on page 140.)* To protect the stone walls, the scaffolding was not anchored in the marble. Instead, supports tipped with rubber pads were snugged up to the walls, giving the scaffolding the necessary degree of support without marring the monument's exterior.

The Monument's Pedigree

Robert Mills, the man who created the original design for the Washington Monument, was an accomplished architect who had worked on many famous buildings in and around Washington,D.C. Born in August, 1781, in Charleston, South Carolina, Mills studied under architect James Hoban, the architect who designed the White House.

From 1802-1809, Mills worked as a draftsman on the design of the U.S. Capitol and the Baltimore Cathedral

$\longrightarrow$

under Benjamin Latrobe. In 1814 Mills received national recognition when he won the competition for the design of Baltimore's Washington Monument. In 1836 he won the competition for the design of the U.S. Treasury building and began a long career as an architect for the federal government. It was during this time that Mills designed the buildings for which he is most widely known: the Post Office and the Washington National Monument. He also supervised construction of the Patent Office and submitted preliminary designs for the Capitol extension and the Smithsonian Institution. He served under seven Presidents. Mills died in 1855.

Thomas Lincoln Casey, the Army engineer who completed the monument, was responsible for the monument's final design. Born in Sackett's Harbor, N.Y., to a military family in 1831, Casey graduated from West Point in 1852 and was assigned to the Corps of Engineers. When the Civil War broke out , Casey was placed in charge of building defenses along the coast of Maine. Following the war, he headed the Corps's division of fortifications.

In 1877, Casey was named Engineer in Charge of Public Buildings and Grounds in Washington, D.C. In this position, Casey directed the construction of several important public buildings in the capital, including the State, War and Navy Building, now called the Old Executive Office Building, located immediately to the west of the White House. He was also given the task of completing the Washington Monument.

In 1888, with the monument completed, Casey was relieved of his position, but in July of that year, he was promoted to brigadier general and named Chief of the Corps of Engineers. Before he died in 1896, Casey supervised the construction of another Washington landmark, the ornate Jefferson Building at the Library of Congress.

Security

The growing threat of terrorism let to new security measures at the Washington Monument beginning in the late 1990's.

In 1998, U.S. Park Police began hand-searching visitors' bags. A tent was erected at the entrance to the monument for this purpose. Metal detectors were later added to the screening process and the tent was replaced by a small structure in 2002.

About the same time the inspections began, concrete New Jersey barriers were placed in a double ring around the base of the monument. The barriers were a temporary measure to protect the monument from a terrorist truck bomb.

In 2005, after much study and discussion, the concrete barriers were removed. New sunken walkways, lined by stone walls, now serve to protect the monument from vehicular attack, while preserving the aesthetics of the grounds.

Following the Tractor Man incident of 2003 (see box below) the Park Police installed surveillance cameras in the monument's observation deck. While the monument provides a convenient pedestal, the addition of the cameras required blocking off half of the eight small windows looking out over the city, creating very crowded conditions at the monument's top level.

The cameras were later removed.

Tractor Man

In the early morning hours of March 18, 2003, North Carolina farmer Dwight W. Watson drove his Jeep along Constitution Avenue in Washington, towing a trailer carrying a green John Deere tractor. Just northwest of the Washington Monument grounds, Watson suddenly turned his rig off the street and into a pond in a part of the Mall known as Constitution Gardens. Watson mounted his tractor, and drove it around in the shallow water. When police arrived, he told them he was protesting the treatment he and his fellow tobacco farmers were receiving from the federal government. He also said he had a bomb on his tractor. That began a 47-hour standoff that closed nearby buildings and snarled traffic. When Watson finally surrendered, police found no explosives in his possession. Watson served 16 months in jail.

Chapter Two:

Watch for Falling (and Flying) Objects

The eight windows of the observation deck at the monument's 500-ft. level are kept closed and locked today to help the air conditioning system maintain a comfortable temperature for visitors. Locking the windows also mitigates the risk of injuries to people below from objects accidentally dropped or deliberately thrown from the top of the tower. Still, the monument's history is full of stories of falling and flying objects.

The Flying Cat

One of the most unusual stories of the Washington Monument is the story of the cat that jumped from the top of the monument, and survived...briefly.

On September 22, 1880, the monument was up to only 160 feet of its eventual 555-foot height. That night, according to a 1927 *Washington Post* article, a cat named Steve Brodie, owned by Mrs. R. E. Brown of Washington, climbed to the top of the construction scaffolding and went to sleep. When the workmen arrived the next morning, they startled the cat. In its eagerness to escape, the frightened cat leapt from the 16-story tower. Witnesses said the animal spread out its paws, flattened its body, and glided like a flying squirrel. The cat hit the ground on all fours, tumbled over a few times, and righted itself, dazed but very much alive.

The cat's leap to safety was short-lived, however (as was the cat). After surviving its 160-foot plunge, Steve Brodie headed for home and the safety of Mrs. Brown. On the way, the cat caught the eye of a neighborhood dog, which chased, caught and killed it. Brodie's incredible luck had run out.

According to another account of the event, cat and dog met on the monument grounds, shortly after the historic leap. The workers who witnessed the cat's amazing feat and untimely death recovered the body and donated it to the Smithsonian Institution, which had the cat stuffed and mounted and placed on display as the only living creature known to have survived a jump from the top of the Washington Monument.

Attempts to verify this story have been futile. The Smithsonian has no record of receiving this particular cat for its collection or putting such an animal on display. According to staff at the Museum of Natural History, the museum has had any number of domestic cats donated, but none specifically designated as the famous flying cat.

About the only fact that could be verified is the existence of the cat's owner. The Washington city directory of the time lists a Patent Office clerk named R.E. Brown living at 720 5th St. NW.

Like the story of Mrs. O'Leary's cow starting the Great Chicago Fire, the leap of Mrs. Brown's cat from the top of the Washington Monument may be just another interesting, but untrue, urban legend.

Tito, the Flying Chihuahua

While the account of the flying cat may be hard to verify, that is not the case with the story of Tito, the dog who took his own unscheduled flight a matter of miles south of the Washington Monument.

Travel about 10 miles in any direction from the monument grounds and you will come to the Capital Beltway, a double ribbon of concrete encircling Washington, D.C., and the inner suburbs of Virginia and Maryland. Officially designated Interstate 495, the eastern third of the beltway also carries Interstate 95, the main north-south Interstate corridor along the East Coast.

On April 6, 1999, Donald and Theresa Holtkamp, a truck-driving couple from Pearson, Ga., were southbound on I-95 near Alexandria, Va., hauling a section of a modular home. Suddenly, a car crossed into their lane. Swerving to avoid a collision, the Holtkamps' rig slammed into a concrete barrier.

———▶

Both Donald and Theresa suffered broken bones and were taken to a local hospital. However, what concerned the couple most was the fate of their pet Chihuahua, Tito. Tito was riding in the truck's cab at the time of the crash, but no one could find the little dog after the accident.

According to reports in the *Washington Post*, members of the Animal Welfare League of Alexandria mobilized to find Tito. They knocked on doors and papered the neighborhood with fliers asking for information. Tito was found two days later, about a half-mile from the scene of the accident. The Holtkamps were overjoyed to hear that their pet had survived the accident and would soon be reunited with them.

What puzzled everyone, however, was that Tito was found on the side of the Beltway away from the accident. To get there, the little dog would have had to cross several lanes of dense, high-speed traffic. It is doubtful that the animal could have survived crossing the Beltway on foot.

Police surmised that Tito didn't run across the Beltway. He flew across it. The impact of the collision must have thrown the dog through the open window of the cab. Like a canine cannonball, Tito was propelled over the treacherous traffic, landing safely in the grass on the other side of the highway, where he stayed until searchers found him.

An Unlucky Break

The most serious injury resulting from an object dropped or thrown from a monument window was a broken wrist suffered by Kathryn Carr of Philadelphia in 1957. While waiting on one of the benches outside the monument for her turn on the elevator, Carr was struck in the right wrist by a telephoto lens dropped from the building's observation deck.

According to the *Washington Post's* account, the two-pound lens had fallen out of the camera of a sailor from Anacostia Naval Air Station.

Carr was taken to a local hospital, where she was treated and released. The expensive lens was not damaged.

Hold onto Your Marbles

In 1954, a 24-year-old woman escaped serious injury when she was struck in the shoulder by a marble apparently dropped from the top of the monument. Mrs. Jean C. Weber of Rockville, Conn., was sitting on a bench outside the monument, waiting for her turn on the elevator, when she felt a sudden, sharp pain in her shoulder. At the same time, she heard a glass marble strike the ground near her feet.

Mrs. Weber was taken to a local hospital where she was treated for a contusion and released.

Officials said they believed the marble may have been tossed out of the window by one of a group of 60 schoolchildren visiting the monument at the time of the incident.

Vitamin C the Hard Way

Stephen Jones and his family from Utica, N.Y., came to visit the Washington Monument on the morning of April 5, 1959. As the nine-year-old boy and his parents waited in line, eagerly awaiting their turn to enter the monument, Stephen was suddenly knocked to the ground by a sharp blow to his chest.

He had been struck by a falling orange.

Stephen was not seriously hurt, just had the wind knocked out of him and suffered a bruise. To be safe, however, he was taken to the hospital, where he was given a clean bill of health. Stephen said it sounded like he had been hit by a wet towel. And Stephen, his parents, and two soldiers waiting behind them in line were all sprayed with orange juice, pulp and rind.

It is not known who tossed the orange out the monument window. However, it is likely that the perpetrator learned of the consequences of the act upon returning to ground level, but did not own up to the deed.

Government-Issued Ammunition

Of the many objects tossed out the monument's windows, rifle shells were among the most common.

For a time, visitors touring the Federal Bureau of Investigation's headquarters were treated to a firing demonstration of various weapons and given the expended shell casings as souvenirs. Many of these tourists, visiting the Washington Monument later in the day, found another use for the shells— tossing or dropping them from the top of the tower.

Play Ball!

In 1908, Washington Senators catcher Charles "Gabby" Street became the first person on record to catch a baseball thrown from the top of the monument. Street's catch settled a $500 bet between Preston Gibson and John Biddle, two local businessmen.

Gibson positioned himself at the top of the monument and rolled a series of baseballs down a wooden chute extended out one of the monument's open windows. The chute was employed to help the baseballs clear the structure's outward-slanting walls. The first several attempts failed because the chute did not project the balls far enough and they kept striking the side of the monument. Eventually, Gibson abandoned the chute and tossed the balls out the window by hand. One of the baseballs managed to clear the building, and Street, decked out in full catcher's gear, caught it.

The ball was later sold at a war bond auction for $40,000.

Street's claim to be the first to perform this feat has been questioned. In 1894, two players from the Chicago Colts (later to become the Cubs), Clark Griffith and William "Pop" Shriver, were in Washington for a National League game against the Washington Nationals. For their own amusement, the two players decided to play a game of vertical catch at the monument. Griffith, a pitcher, went to the top of the monument, while Shriver, his catcher, awaited the toss. According to the *Washington Post* of August 26, 1894, Shriver let the first ball drop, but caught the second.

However, Griffith, who went on to become the owner of the Washington Senators of the American League, later wrote in his book on the history of the franchise that Shriver dropped both attempts

Charles (Gabby) Street

Gabby Street, traded from Washington to New York for first baseman Jack Knight, first donned the mask and big glove in his home town at Huntsville, Ala., in 1901. From Huntsville he next started with Clarksville in the Kentucky - Tennessee League in 1903, and from there went to Terre Haute, Cincinnati, San Francisco and back to Washington. He is now Ford's battery partner with New York, although he won fame at Washington where, in 1911, he hit .222, fielded .973, and caught a ball tossed from the top of Washington Monument.

Recruit
LITTLE CIGARS

FACTORY N° 240. 1ST DIST. PA.

Catcher Charles "Gabby" Street of the Washington Senators, shown above in a 1911 baseball card issued by the American Tobacco Co., is reputed to be the first person to catch a baseball tossed from the top of the Washington Monument. The back of a 1912 card, issued after Street had been traded to New York, tells of his historic catch.

before the stunt was interrupted by a guard. In its reporting of Street's catch of 1908, the *Post* agreed with Griffith and gave Street the credit for making the first catch.

There's another mystery associated with Street's catch. Years after the event, it was noticed that the ball from the famous catch was a National League model. This puzzled baseball fans, since Street played for the Senators of the American League.

Street's daughter, Sally Street Hall, explained that Gibson had taken a box of 12 American League balls with him to the top of the monument and used them all on the wooden chute. When the supply was exhausted, Gibson put the chute down, pulled a 13th ball from his pocket and threw it out the window. According to Mrs. Hall, that 13th ball happened to be a National League model, and that was the ball Street caught.

The First Shall Be Last

When President Washington died in 1799, his friend and Revolutionary War colleague Henry "Light Horse Harry" Lee eulogized the First President as "First in war, first in peace, and first in the hearts of his countrymen."

A hundred years later, vaudeville comics lampooned the hapless Washington, D.C. baseball franchise, calling the city "First in war, first in peace and last in the National League."

The Washington club, known as the Nationals, was so bad, it was one of four franchises dropped when the league pared down from 12 to eight teams in 1899. When the upstart American League formed in 1901, Washington was awarded a franchise and the new team kept the Nationals nickname for a time, but later became known as the Washington Senators.

After 1901, then, the comics had to change their opinion of Washington baseball. The town was no longer last in the National League. It was now last in the American League. Washington shed that distinction in 1971, when the Senators left town and became the Texas Rangers. In 2005, National League baseball returned to the capital when the Montreal Expos moved to town and became the Washington Nationals. In their inaugural season in D.C., the Nationals finished last.

I Got It! I Got It! Ouch!

In 1952, the famous comic feature "Ripley's Believe It or Not" told the story of another baseball catch at the monument. Robert Baker caught a ball tossed from the top of the tower, but, unlike Street, Baker did not wear a glove. His barehanded catch earned Baker a place in the Believe It or Not archives, and two broken knuckles.

Diamonds on the Mall:
Baseball on the Monument Grounds

Although Gabby Street is reputed to be the first person to catch a baseball dropped from the top of the Washington Monument, baseball was no stranger to the monument grounds. The game came to the monument more than 40 years before Street made his catch in 1908.

In the years following the Civil War, a number of baseball clubs took up residence on the monument grounds, even maintaining clubhouses on the grounds. Monument records show a team named the PMGO (Paymaster General's Office) Base Ball Club using the grounds as early as April, 1865, as the war drew to a close. Other clubs to have home field advantage on the monument grounds between 1865 and 1870 included the Interior (Department) Base Ball Club, Capitol Base Ball Club, and the Arlington Base Ball Club.

Today, summer evenings find the Washington Monument grounds populated with co-ed softball teams from Capitol Hill, downtown lobbying firms and federal departments and agencies. Where the PMGO club and the others once played, we find teams with names such as Crude and Unrefined (Dept. of Energy), the Accidental Tourists (Tourism Industry Association) and the Minnesota Knee-Jerk Liberals (three Democratic offices from that state).

Ice Cream and Opera and Baseball and Politics

What could have been the most unusual item to be tossed from the monument windows never made the trip. On March 26, 1954, the *Washington Daily News* reported that Congressman Carroll Kearns, a Pennsylvania Republican, wanted to drop a bill he had just introduced from the top of the monument. Stranger still, he had wrapped the bill around a scoop of ice cream.

The bill called for the appropriation of funds to construct a memorial opera house in Washington, D.C. It had nothing to do with the Washington Monument, baseball, or, for that matter, ice cream. Still, the gentleman from Pennsylvania wanted to drop it from the monument.

The superintendent of the monument dissuaded the Congressman from tossing his concoction of legislation and cold confection from the top of the building. Instead, Kearns settled for a photo opportunity. He posed for news photographers holding his bill (with the ice cream inside) like a baseball pitcher ready to throw. A radio announcer posed as a catcher waiting for the pitch, and the monument's superintendent took the position of the home plate umpire.

News accounts of the day did not report if Kearns fired his press secretary when he returned to Capitol Hill.

Flower Power

Washington, D.C., was showered with flowers and money on September 5, 1951. In a promotion for F.T.D. florists, 200 orchids, worth $3,000, were thrown from the monument windows. In addition, the florists released 20 balloons bearing ribbons entitling the finder to a $25 defense bond.

"Just like Superman"

People were among the objects flying about the monument on February 26, 1961.

As reported in the *Washington Post* the next day, wind gusts reaching 59 miles per hour lifted some visitors to the monument grounds off their feet and carried them several yards through the air.

Others were knocked down by the wind. Three people were hospitalized, three others were treated for minor injuries.

"I felt just like Superman," said Janine Bishop, 15, of West Bridgewater, Mass., who was lifted off her feet and carried 20 feet through the air.

A mother and daughter from Carlisle, Pa., were among those hospitalized. Jeanne Gibbs and her 11-year-old daughter, Cynthia, were treated for possible concussions and numerous bruises, after being carried some 50 feet by the wind and hurled into a lamp post.

People stayed put, but plywood flew at the monument on July 21, 1998, when a sudden storm brought strong gusts. At the time, the monument was surrounded by a plywood wall in preparation for upcoming renovations. The heavy gusts pulled several plywood panels away from the fence and sent them flying around the grounds. According to the *Washington Post*, a panel struck one of the 50 aluminum flagpoles surrounding the monument, shearing it off.

Even though the monument site is normally filled with visitors on a typical July evening, no serious injuries resulted. Rangers had closed the monument and sent away visitors when the storm hit. About 20 people took refuge inside the monument until the storm passed.

Strong winds at the monument are not unusual. The monument stands atop a hill with few obstructions to block or divert the wind. Moreover, the monument itself acts as a giant airfoil, forcing the air to accelerate as it flows around the massive tower. That is why rangers now close the monument when extreme winds kick up.

The World's Largest Flagstaff

A prominent building such as the Washington Monument makes a tempting location for those trying to promote a cause, and several activists have yielded to the temptation. On two such occasions, the monument served briefly as the world's largest flagstaff.

On May 15, 1960, Polish immigrant Jozef Miloz Mraz unfurled a 110-foot black shroud in a gesture to protest Communist rule in Poland. Mraz, of Salem, Mass., was identified in the *Washington Post* as a "graduate of German and Russian prison camps." According to the news account, Mraz identified himself as the president of a group called Anti-Communist Confederation of Polish Freedom-Fighters of the U.S.A., and said he was in Washington to protest communism.

Mraz said he had hidden inside the monument and waited for the building to close. He was charged with damage to government property, but the charge was later dropped.

Students from Washington, D.C.'s Gonzaga High School came to the monument with a lighter purpose. On November 22, 1957, before a game against rival St. John's, the students unfurled a banner reading "Beat St. John's" from one of the monument's windows. The stunt didn't help their team's cause, however. Two days later at Griffith Stadium, St. John's beat Gonzaga, 33-7.

The Washington Monument almost became the staff for the world's largest flag. In 1980, a patriotic Vermont businessman named Len Silverfine brought a massive American flag to the monument to celebrate Flag Day. Silverfine's flag measured 411 ft. by 210 ft. (For comparison, a standard American football field is 300 ft. long and 160.5 ft. wide.) The flag weighed seven tons and each star was 13 ft. point-to-point.

Silverfine, who had a reputation for thinking big, came up with the idea for the flag during the U.S. Bicentennial Year, 1976, when he had a 71,000 square-foot flag made and suspended from New York's Verrazano Narrows Bridge. Unfortunately, the winds whistling past the famous bridge destroyed the flag, but not Silverfine's dream.

In 1980, Silverfine had a new flag made of sturdier fabric, but the Bicentennial celebration was long over and the enthusiasm for the big flag waned. Still, Silverfine had big plans. He envisioned his big flag flying from the Washington Monument on Flag Day. The National Park Service, however, said no. The big flag nevertheless did participate in the Flag Day festivities. Silverfine, with the help of a large number of tourists recruited at the last minute, unfurled his banner on the monument grounds in time for the Flag Day parade.

In 1983, Silverfine presented the flag to President Ronald Reagan. Much to his disappointment, the federal government made little use of the flag. Silverfine hoped the flag would be displayed every Flag Day. It was displayed again on the Washington Monument grounds only one more time, in 1991. Silverfine's flag was eventually declared surplus property by the government and sold to an aerospace museum in Kansas.

Another, even larger flag came to the monument grounds on Flag Day, 1993. According to the *Washington Post*, the nylon flag measured 505 ft. by 255 ft. Its owner was Thomas "Ski" Demski of Long Beach, Calif. Demski, a former mayor of Long Beach, owned several large American flags. He had this particular one made when he read that the Chinese owned the largest flag in the world. Demski felt that the record belonged in America. Demski's big flag won a place in the *Guinness Book of World Records*, and brought the record home.

It's a Bird! It's a Plane! It's a Blimp!

In 1932, the U.S. Army came up with a unique way to honor George Washington on his 200th birthday. The Army delivered a large wreath to the Washington Monument using a blimp.

Despite having to dodge a few trees and light poles, the blimp's pilot managed to land the airship near the base of the monument and delivered the wreath on time and on target.

High Notes

The strains of opera once echoed from the top of the Washington Monument. Dr. Alfredo Warsaw, a singer with the Metropolitan Opera, sang from the top of the monument in 1910. In 1948, Warsaw took his act even higher when he sang from the top of New York's Empire State Building.

Baritone Phil O'Brien and accordionist Milton Dains shared their performance from the top of the monument with a local radio audience in 1934. The pair was part of a broadcast hosted by announcer Ted Kimball of station WMAL.

The broadcast was arranged by the Park Service to assure the public that the monument was structurally sound, even though it was undergoing repairs at the time.

In 1946, trumpeter Lloyd Geisler of the National Symphony Orchestra played Beethoven's "Lenore Overture No. 3" from the monument's window. Geisler performed the stunt to mark the 10th anniversary of the symphony's outdoor concerts on the Potomac riverfront.

According to the *Washington Times-Herald*, Geisler's music could be heard clearly on Constitution Avenue, at the northern edge of the monument grounds. Closer to the source, however, it was a different story. People waiting for the elevator at the foot of the monument were unaware of the music being played 500 feet above.

The classical music must have gone over their heads.

*An Army blimp delivered a wreath to the Washington
Monument as part of the observance of the 200th anniversary of
George Washington's birth in February, 1932.*

The World On a String

Kite flying is a popular activity on the Washington Monument grounds, but it wasn't always so. At one time, flying a kite near the monument was illegal.

That changed in 1967. Paul E. Garber, legendary curator of the National Air and Space Museum, along with a number of kite enthusiasts, challenged the law and gave birth to the annual Smithsonian Kite Festival.

Held on the last Saturday in March, the festival regularly draws some 150 kite enthusiasts and hundreds of spectators to the monument grounds. Participants have come from as far away as Japan.

The kites can range from the ordinary to the spectacular. Past festivals have included creations such as a 100-foot-long octopus with tentacles that rippled in the wind. In 1997, local kite clubs joined forces to create a string of 150 diamond kites to honor the Smithsonian on its 150th anniversary.

Though kite flying is now allowed on the Washington Monument grounds, there are still limits. Kites cannot fly higher than 550 feet, so as not to extend higher than the 555-foot monument.

Time to Say "G'Day!"

Boomerangs flew about the Washington Monument in 1970, thanks to the Smithsonian Institution.

The Smithsonian conducted a series of four weekend workshops on boomerang throwing for members of the Smithsonian Associates program.

The event was the brainchild of Benjamin Ruhe, a publicist for the Institution. Ruhe had grown up in New South Wales, Australia, where he learned the "ancient and honorable art" of the boomerang.

Ruhe provided instruction for participants, who then competed for trophies.

Chapter Three:

Stories in Stone

The interior walls of the 555-foot monument are lined with 194 memorial stones. These stones were collected from a wide variety of donors, including states and foreign governments, private individuals and Masonic lodges, Sunday schools and fire departments.

In 1849, when the monument was in its earliest stages of construction, a group of citizens from Alabama proposed a donation of marble from their state to the monument project. This offer led the Washington National Monument Society to invite all the states and territories to donate stones to the project, in the hope that these donations would spur interest in the monument, and revitalize lagging subscriptions. Later, the society extended the invitation to Native American tribes, social and fraternal organizations, local communities, trade unions and other groups and individuals. It also invited American diplomats abroad to seek stones from foreign governments, as a gesture of respect for George Washington and friendship with the United States.

The memorial stones decorate the walls along the monument's staircase from the 30-ft. level to the 450-ft. level, and form a patchwork of tributes to Washington. Taken as a whole, the stones weave the remarkable story of our first President, his monument, and the nation he did so much to establish.

These commemorative stones are best viewed from the monument's interior staircase, although passengers on the elevator can now catch a glimpse at some of the stones, thanks to new glass doors that become transparent as the elevator descends. The stairway was once open to the public, but since 1976 the National Park Service has restricted access to the stairs to guided tours given by park rangers or trained volunteers.

The Million Dollar Baby

The first of the 194 commemorative stones that visitors see when descending the monument's staircase is at the 450-ft. level, the stone donated by the State of Alaska. The Alaska stone is also reputed to be the most valuable. Carved from a solid block of jade from Alaska's Jade Mountain, the stone is valued by the Park Service at an estimated "several million dollars." The Alaska stone is also the newest from any of the 50 states. It was installed on February 8, 1982, and dedicated on February 22, George Washington's 250th birthday.

Alaska Come Lately

Alaska may have been the 49th state to enter the Union, but it was the 50th to provide a stone to the Washington Monument. Hawaii, which became a state in August of 1959, seven months after Alaska, had donated a stone while it was still a territory.

It wasn't until Alaska and Hawaii sought representation at the Lincoln Memorial—which has the names of the 48 states in the Union when the Memorial was dedicated inscribed on its upper walls—that the 49th state awoke to the fact that it was the only state not represented in the Washington Monument.

The Pope and the Know Nothings

At the 340-ft. level is a block of white Carrera marble with the inscription "A Roma Americae," Latin for "From Rome to America." This is the Pope's Stone, or more accurately, Pope's Stone II. The original Pope's Stone was stolen from the monument grounds in March,1854, by a political faction known as the "Know Nothings."

The Know Nothings were members of a loosely constituted political party, officially called the American Party. The party's membership were Nativists, native-born Protestants who had developed a suspicion and dislike for the new waves of Catholic immigrants coming to America in the mid-19th Century.

Pope Pius IX was among the foreign dignitaries who donated commemorative stones to be placed in the Washington Monument. The Pope sent a marble block carved from the ancient Roman Temple of Concord as a gesture of friendship to the United States and a tribute to George Washington.

The Pope's gift, however, was viewed as something sinister by the American Party and other anti-Catholic factions in the country. Petitions circulated in New Jersey and Pennsylvania and elsewhere contended that the message, "From Rome to America," carried "a significance beyond its natural meaning." Perhaps they saw it as a pledge that the Pope himself planned to relocate his Holy See from Rome to America. The Pope's Stone was decried as a "gift of a despot," which, if installed in the monument, "can never be looked upon by true Americans, but with feelings of mortification and disgust."

So strong were their views on this issue that on March 6, 1854, a group of local Know Nothings decided to take matters into their own hands. That night, a small band of masked men sneaked onto the monument grounds, and broke into the storage shed where the Pope's Stone was awaiting installation. They trapped the night watchman in his guard booth and held him there at gunpoint. (There later was some suspicion that the watchman was actually in on the plan.)

They tossed the Pope's Stone into a handcart, rolled it down to the bank of Potomac River, where a boat was waiting. The thieves broke the stone into pieces, rowed it out into the middle of the river and dropped the pieces overboard near the current location of the 14th Street Bridge.

In 1982, through the efforts of Father James Grant of Spokane, Wash., a new Pope's Stone was installed, returning the Pope's tribute to America 128 years after the Know Nothings' raid.

One further note: If the Know Nothings' goal was to keep the Pope away from America, they were too late. Pope Pius IX, who donated the original Pope's Stone, became the first Pontiff to set foot on American territory. In 1849, the Pope was a guest aboard the frigate *U.S.S. Constitution* ("Old Ironsides") while the ship was anchored at Naples, Italy, during an international goodwill tour.

Father James Grant of Spokane, Wash. donated this stone in 1982 to replace a stone sent by Pope Pius IX. The original Pope's stone was stolen in 1854 by members of an anti-Catholic group called the "Know Nothings." The replacement stone is at the monument's 340-ft. level.

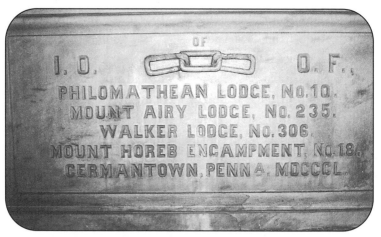

Several stones sent by lodges of the Independent Order of Odd Fellows (I. O. O. F.) show the Odd Fellows symbol of a chain with three links. The links represent friendship, love and truth.

One Man's Faith, Work, and Generosity

Father James Grant was in Washington, D.C., on sabbatical in 1980 and, like most other visitors to the capital, took in the monuments, museums and other sights of the city. While on a visit to the Washington Monument, Father Grant heard the story of the Know Nothings and the theft of the Pope's Stone. The priest from Spokane felt a need to undo this outrageous act and got to work to have a new Pope's Stone installed in the monument.

Father Grant researched the story of the 1854 raid and learned the original stone's size, color and inscription. He contacted the National Park Service and won permission to have a new stone installed. Then Father Grant ordered a marble block of proper color and dimensions from a Spokane stonecutter. (He did make one concession. According to records, the original Pope's Stone was 10 inches thick. At the request of the Park Service, Father Grant had the new stone cut only six inches thick.) The priest had the block inscribed with the original stone's message, "*A Roma Americae*" (From Rome to America), and shipped it to Washington.

When the bill came due for the cost of this project, Father Grant paid for it out of his own pocket. When he was interviewed for this book, Father Grant would not say how much he had spent. "It wasn't too much, but it wasn't too little, either," was all he would say on the subject.

The new Pope's Stone was installed on November 16, 1982. The Know Nothings were finally thwarted. The Pope's message of friendship had come back to the Washington Monument thanks to the faith, work, and generosity of one individual, not a wealthy New York industrialist or powerful Washington politician, but a humble Catholic priest from Spokane, Father James Grant.

Does the Smithsonian
Have a Piece of the Pope's Stone?

In 1972, Kathryn Wells of Oxon Hill, Md., gave the Smithsonian Institution a 20-inch obelisk she claimed was carved from the original Pope's Stone by one of the Know-Nothing conspirators. Ms. Wells claimed she was given the carving in 1911 by a friend, Joseph Ridgway, who had served as a captain in the Confederate Army. Capt. Ridgway told Ms. Wells that his brother was one of the conspirators and that another one of the Know Nothings had actually carved the stone. Ms. Wells had kept the carving secretly locked away in a closet for more than 60 years. She didn't even tell her family of its existence, until she decided to donate the stone to the Smithsonian.

The authenticity of the obelisk is questionable. The carving is of red variegated marble, but descriptions of the original Pope's Stone refer to its color as "white," "cream-colored," or "black and gray." No trace of the Temple of Concord exists, so there is no way to compare the obelisk with the marble used in the temple.

I Once Was Lost, But Now I'm Found

In 1855, Dr. David Porter Heap, son of the U.S. Consul in Tunis, North Africa, sent a stone for the monument with a diplomatic shipment. The stone was cut from one of the columns of the Temple of Esculapius in the ancient city of Carthage. The stone was of variegated red and white marble, and its face bore a mosaic design depicting a horse and palm tree, and attribution to Dr. Heap.

What happened to the Carthage stone after its arrival is filled with mystery. An 1886 inventory of the commemorative pieces lists the Carthage stone as being located in the "northwest corner of the monument in the floor" at the 260-foot landing. An 1888 letter soliciting bids from contractors to install the remaining memorial stones in the building originally listed the Carthage stone as one of those waiting for installation, but the entry was later crossed out. No reason for deleting the Carthage stone from that list was given.

When the Park Service installed a new elevator in 1959, workers discovered the Carthage stone at the bottom of the elevator shaft. How it got there, no one knows. The stone was then placed on a shelf above the northeast staircase leading from the observation area at the 500-ft.level to the elevator lobby and bookstore one level below.

During the 1999 restoration Carthage stone was finally installed at the 380-ft. level in the monument's interior wall with the rest of the commemorative stones, 144 years after its donation by Dr. Heap.

I Once Was Lost, but Now I'm...Still Lost!

Other stones that were to be displayed in the Washington Monument weren't as lucky as the Carthage Stone. They were lost and have never been recovered. They include:

✱ A 2,000-year-old block from the Temple of Augustus in Egypt;

✱ A stone removed from a 1388 chapel in Switzerland dedicated to the Swiss hero William Tell;

✱ A block cut from a temple on the Greek Island of Paros by officers of the U.S. warship *USS Saranac*; and

✱ A three-foot slab of granite inscribed only with the letter G, from an unknown donor.

Three others listed on the 1872 inventory are also missing. The first was a stone cut from Italy's Mt. Vesuvius donated by William Ferrel of Georgia. The second stone was an "ancient Egyptian head presented by J.D. Lehman."

The third was a stone from the Looshoo Islands, today known as the Ryukyu Islands, a part of the Japanese province of Okinawa. The stone was presented to Commodore Matthew C. Perry in 1854, but never reached the monument.

In 1984, a visitor from Japan asked to see the stone given to Perry. Park Rangers could not locate the stone. So, in 1989, the National Park Service accepted a replacement stone from the people of Okinawa, Prefecture of Japan, to replace the one that was sent 135 years earlier. The Ryukyu Islands Stone, a block of polished coral bearing a message—in English and Japanese—of tribute to George Washington and friendship to the people of the United States was installed at the 310-ft. level. It is the newest memorial stone in the monument. The fate of Perry's original contribution is unknown.

Lost, Found, then Lost Again

Donations of memorial stones by foreign countries for the Washington Monument were usually the work of U.S. diplomats and naval officers abroad. At the time George W. Kimball was the U.S. Consul to the British island of St. Helena, where the French Emperor Napoleon spent his final days, Kimball thought the monument should have a stone taken from Napoleon's tomb located on the island. After prolonged negotiations with the French government and Emperor Napoleon III, Kimball obtained a stone for the Washington Monument. (Although the island was ruled by Britain, the tomb was under the control of France.) The stone was crated with great ceremony and shipped to America on the Navy ship *USS Mystic* in 1860.

Records show the stone made it as far as Washington, but never made it into the monument. In late 1861, the commandant of the Brooklyn Navy Yard wrote that once the stone had been unloaded from the *Mystic,* its shipment to Washington had been overlooked. He reported that the stone had been located and prepared for transport to Washington.

However, shipping the Napoleon stone to the monument was not the Navy's top priority at the time. The Civil War was underway and the Navy had to devote its attention to the war effort. Again, the stone was forgotten.

In 1880, 20 years after it was shipped from St. Helena, another attempt was made to locate the stone from Napoleon's tomb. However, the passage of time and the demands of the war made it difficult to trace the stone's fate. Then, on April 21, 1880, the commandant of the Washington Navy Yard reported that the "stone is in this yard subject to the disposition of the National Monument Association." The stone from Napoleon's tomb is included in the 1888 inventory of stones still to be added to the monument, but it was never installed.

An even more dramatic fate befell a stone shipped from the gold fields of California. On June 20, 1860, the Monument Society received a letter from Herbert J. Bennett, a salvor who had been recovering cargo from the wreck of the *Flying Dutchman* off the New Jersey coast. One of the items Bennett and his crew recovered was a block of stone bearing the inscription, "Miners of Columbia, Touloume Co., Calif., To the Father of the Country, July 4, 1857." The stone bore a gold quartz star in each corner.

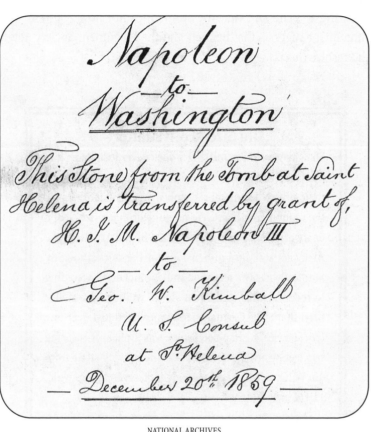

*Despite the best efforts of the U.S. Navy and George Kimball,
U.S. Consul to the island of St. Helena, the stone taken
from the tomb of Napoleon never made it into the Washington
Monument. The inscription Kimball composed for
the stone is illustrated here.*

In a subsequent letter, Bennett reported that the block was in Atlantic City, and promised to send it on to Washington. Although Bennett said he would ship the stone at no cost, he later hinted at obtaining some sort of compensation for the expenses he incurred recovering it. The fact that the stone does not now reside in the monument suggests that Bennett and the Monument Society never did resolve this issue.

Did Size Really Matter?

So, why were these missing stones never installed? It is possible that they were eventually rejected because of their size. When memorial stones were first accepted for the monument, there were no guidelines for size, shape or inscriptions. In the later years of construction, the Army set standard dimensions for the stones, roughly four feet wide, two feet high, and one foot deep. According to records, most of the lost stones were much smaller than that. The Carthage stone measures just over one foot square. The Napoleon stone was listed as measuring two feet by one foot, five inches. The missing stone from the William Tell chapel was one foot, seven inches wide, 11 1/4 inches high.

Another factor may have been a lack of inscription on some of the stones. The stone from Napoleon's tomb was delivered without an inscription. Kimball sent a suggested text and design for the inscription, but the stone itself was shipped blank. Other stones in the inventory were listed as "rough block, no inscription," and "no inscription, probably from Texas or some other state."

As the Corps of Engineers put the finishing touches on the monument, a decision may have been made to eliminate the smaller stones and the blank stones in favor of expediency and conformity. Of these smaller stones, only the Carthage stone survived.

Braddock's Field
A Turning Point in History

At the base of the stairway at the 240-ft. level is a granite stone bearing the inscription "From Braddock's Field." The stone comes from the site of a battle during the French and Indian War (1754-1763). (In Europe, this was known as the Seven Years' War. However, in North America it took nine years to fight the Seven Years' War, so we call it the French and Indian War.)

In the mid-18th Century, the North American continent was being carved up and colonized by the major European powers: Spain, France and Great Britain. The Spanish claimed Florida and the Southwest, the British controlled most of the Atlantic coast, the French held Canada and the Mississippi Valley. Britain and France both claimed title to the Ohio River valley, which lay between their holdings.

The French pressed their claim to the Ohio territory by building several fortifications. In early 1754 they occupied the forks of the Ohio River and built a fort on the site. They called it Fort Duquesne. The British protested this French intrusion into lands claimed by Virginia colony, but the French refused to withdraw. So, in April of 1754 Governor Robert Dinwiddie of Virginia sent an expeditionary force into the Ohio Territory. The force included young George Washington, who at the time was 22 years old and held the rank of lieutenant colonel in the Virginia militia.

The Virginians' mission was three-fold: first, to build a road through the virgin wilderness of Maryland and Pennsylvania and across the Allegheny Mountains to the Ohio Valley—there was no Pennsylvania Turnpike in those days—then, to remove the French presence from the area, and, finally, to establish settlements in the new territory.

J. BERARD

*The Colorado stone, at the monument's 290-foot level, was carved
from the same material as the Tomb of the Unknowns at Arlington
Cemetery. In 1949 a Geiger counter detected a small amount of
radioactivity in the wall beneath the Colorado stone.*

J. BERARD

*The Battle of Braddock's Field during the French
and Indian War had a great impact on the life of young George
Washington and on the future United States of America.*

While en route, Washington's column joined the rest of the Virginia regiment, under the command of Colonel Joshua Fry, who had overall command of the expedition. When Fry died on May 31, Lt. Colonel Washington assumed command.

Washington and his men got as far as what is now Uniontown, Pa., when they ran into trouble with a much larger contingent of French troops and their Native American allies. Out-manned and outgunned, Washington built a defensive stockade he named Fort Necessity, but could not hold out against the superior French force. Washington surrendered Fort Necessity and was allowed to march his troops back to British territory. This was the first, last, and only time in his military career that George Washington surrendered to an enemy force.

A year later, a second expeditionary force consisting of nearly 2,400 British regulars and colonial militiamen under the command of Major General Edward Braddock of the regular British Army, set off to complete the previous year's mission: finish the road, remove the French from the Ohio Valley, and establish British settlements there. General Braddock and his troops came within eight miles of Fort Duquesne when they encountered the enemy.

In the ensuing battle, General Braddock was killed, and his senior officers were all either killed or wounded, as were about two-thirds of the British troops. Command fell once again on the shoulders of Colonel Washington, who was serving as aide de camp to General Braddock. Washington led the surviving troops back to friendly territory. En route, Washington's men buried General Braddock's body near Fort Necessity, the site of Washington's defeat a year earlier. The men buried Braddock in a grave dug in the middle of the road and ran wagons over it in order to disguise its location and prevent desecration by Indians loyal to the French.

The Battle of Braddock's Field was not significant in terms of the outcome of the war. The British overcame the early setbacks at Fort Necessity and Braddock's Field to win the war and capture most of the French holdings in North America. The French abandoned Fort Duquesne in 1758, and the British built their own fort on the site. The British called their fortification Fort Pitt, and the town that sprung up around the fort became known as Pittsburgh, Pennsylvania.

These battles held great significance for Washington's future. Prior to this battle, Washington's main ambition in life was to secure a commission in the regular British Army. Although he held the rank of lieutenant colonel in the militia, Washington felt appointment as an officer in the King's Army was his best route to rising on the social ladder of colonial Virginia. Washington's sponsor for this commission was General Braddock. When Braddock was killed at Braddock's Field, Washington's hopes for that commission died with him.

After the war, Washington abandoned his hopes for a military career and turned his attention to running the family plantation at Mount Vernon. As a gentleman farmer, Washington experienced the trade restrictions the British government had placed on the colonies. This spurred him to enter politics. He was elected to the colonial legislature, the Virginia House of Burgesses, where he met others, such as Patrick Henry, who were similarly disenchanted with Britain's treatment of the American colonists.

When the 13 American colonies openly rebelled against the crown in 1775, they called upon Washington and his military experience to lead the Continental Army against the British. After the war, Washington was called upon to preside over the Constitutional Convention and served as the first President of the United States under the new Constitution.

Beam me up, Scotty!

Any fan of Star Trek knows that history often turns on a single event. This has been the theme of several Star Trek episodes and other films and television shows dealing with time travel. In the original Star Trek series, Dr. McCoy traveled back to the 1930's, saved a young woman's life and unwittingly changed the outcome of the Second World War. In the Star Trek movie, "First Contact," the crew of the Enterprise fights to preserve history by keeping the Borg from sabotaging Earth's first contact with the Vulcans. Other movies, such as "The Terminator," also deal with this theme.

The battle of Braddock's Field is one such turning point. If the Borg or the Terminator wanted to change the course of American history, they might be able to do it by changing the outcome of this battle. Had General Braddock survived, Washington might have won the

$\longrightarrow$

King's commission he wanted so badly, and may not have stepped forward to lead the American colonies to independence.

In fact, Washington could have become the commander of the British forces sent to suppress the rebellion. And it is very possible that today, before each baseball game, Americans would stand to sing "God Save the Queen," instead of "The Star Spangled Banner."

Stand Back! It's Radioactive!

At least one stone on the monument stairway can get the attention of a Geiger counter: the Colorado state stone, at the 290-ft. level. According to an article in the *Washington Times-Herald* on September 2, 1949, a Geiger counter registered a low radiation level (140/sec.) at the Colorado stone.

The Colorado stone was carved from a block of Colorado Yule Marble. This same material, quarried at Marble, Colo., covers the Lincoln Memorial. The Tomb of the Unknowns at Arlington National Cemetery is carved from a solid block of Colorado Yule Marble. It is not known if any similar Geiger counter tests were ever conducted at the Memorial or the Tomb.

The article said the radiation was detected below the Colorado stone, so the stone itself—and, by extension, the Lincoln Memorial and the Tomb of the Unknowns—may not be radioactive. But that then opens the question of why the section of the wall beneath the stone would emit radiation while other areas of the monument wall, made up of the same material, do not.

The Angel and the Fireman

The New York City Fire Department stone at the 260-ft. level is one of the more remarkable stones in the monument. It is larger than most (6 ft. wide, 4 ft., 6 in. high), but it is most interesting for the story that it tells. The figures carved into the white marble stone depict a fireman who died in the line of duty, standing in civilian

J. BERARD

*The New York City Fire Department stone pays tribute
to firefighters who have died in the line of duty. Philadelphia,
Cincinnati and Washington, D.C., fire departments also
donated stones to the monument.*

J. BERARD

*Several church groups, including Sunday school classes, took up
collections to provide a memorial stone to the monument.*

clothes, with his fireman's gear, no longer needed, stashed in the lower left corner. Behind the fireman stands an angel, waiting to escort him to his reward. A seated female figure, representing the City, is handing the fireman a paper marked "discharge certificate," while an inverted torch at her side symbolizes loss. Standing behind the seated figure are a woman and child, dressed in classical toga and tunic, representing the women and children of New York offering their thanks to the fireman who died in their service.

Where's the Fire?

Fire departments in 19th Century America were fraternal organizations as well as city departments. To this day, in many American communities, volunteer fire departments and rescue squads continue that tradition. When the call went out for commemorative stones to be displayed in the Washington Monument, fire departments joined other organizations in sending their tributes to Washington. Fire departments from New York City, Philadelphia, Cincinnati and Washington, D.C., all have stones on display in the monument.

From Teacher to Student

An appropriate tribute to the teaching profession is presented by the stone from the teachers of the Buffalo, N.Y., public schools (250-ft. level). The gray granite block shows one hand passing a torch—a symbol of knowledge—upward to another hand, as the teacher passes knowledge from one generation to the next.

The torch of knowledge can also be seen at another Washington landmark. A gilded torch tops the copper dome of the historic Jefferson Building of the Library of Congress.

The Civil War in Stone

George Washington died December 14, 1799, but many of the stones in the monument, especially stones donated by states that made up the Union in the mid-19th Century, bear inscriptions that reflect less on Washington and his times, and more on the political debate of their own era.

The time of the monument's first phase of construction (1848-1854) was a time of greatly heated debate inflamed by the slavery issue. At the heart of this debate was the question of the relative powers of the federal government balanced against the rights of the sovereign states, and whether the states had the right to secede from the Union if they felt the federal government no longer served their needs.

Tennessee sent a stone bearing a quote from favorite son Andrew Jackson, "The federal union, it must be preserved." Slave state Tennessee would later ignore Jackson's words and leave the Union in favor of the Confederacy. Another slave holding state, Kentucky, trumpeted the compromises hammered out by its own Senators Henry Clay and John T. Crittenden, declaring "Kentucky will be the last to give up the Union." Unlike Tennessee, Kentucky remained true to its pledge. Despite its status as a slave state, and strong Southern ties, Kentucky never officially seceded from the Union and was considered a loyal state by the North throughout the war.

Other states' stones bear inscriptions with similar themes:

✳ Delaware: "The first to adopt will be the last to desert the Constitution"

✳ Georgia: "The Union as it was, the Constitution as it is."

✳ Illinois: "State Sovereignty, National Union"

✳ Indiana: "Knows no North, no South, nothing but the Union."

✳ Iowa: "Her affections, like the rivers of her borders, flow to an inseparable Union."

✳ Michigan: "An emblem of her trust in the Union."

There is also a touch of Civil War irony at the 200-ft. level, where stones from the state of West Virginia and the city of Richmond, Va., are mounted side-by-side. Richmond, the state capital, served as the Confederate capital for most of the Civil War. West Virginia was created by citizens in the mountainous western counties of Virginia, who opposed their state's withdrawal from the Union. In an historic turnabout, they seceded from Virginia and petitioned Congress for

Arizona sent three rings of petrified wood with the name of the state emblazoned in gold leaf. The stone is set in the wall at the monument's 320-ft. level.

ΓΕΩΡΓΙΩ. ΟΥΑΣΙΚΤΩΝΙ

ΗΡΩΙ ΣΤΡΑΤΗΓΩ. ΑΚΡΩ. ΠΟΛΙΤΗ. ΙΔΡΥΤΗ. ΝΕΑΣ ΕΛΕΥΘΕΡΙΑΣ ΕΥΝΟΜΟΥ

Η ΣΟΛΩΝΟΣ ΘΕΜΙΣΤΟΚΛΕΟΥΣ ΠΕΡΙΚΛΕΟΥΣ ΠΑΤΡΙΣ

ΤΗΣ ΑΡΧΑΙΑΣ ΕΛΕΥΘΕΡΙΑΣ ΜΗΤΗΡ

ΤΟΝ ΑΡΧΑΙΟΝ ΤΟΥΤΟΝ ΛΙΘΟΝ

ΤΙΜΗΣ ΚΑΙ ΘΑΥΜΑΣΜΟΥ ΤΕΚΜΗΡΙΟΝ

The king of Greece sent a stone carved from the Parthenon. The inscription calls George Washington "the hero, the citizen of the new and illustrious liberty."

admission to the Union as a separate state. (Congress was only too happy to oblige.) Now the stones from Virginia's capital and her prodigal child share the same wall in tribute to native Virginian George Washington.

Nice Material

Most of the commemorative stones in the monument are carved from a variety of marble, granite, sandstone or limestone. However, a few contributions are cut from more exotic materials:

* Alaska-Jade
* Arizona-Petrified wood
* Okinawa-Coral
* Michigan-Copper
* Minnesota-Catlinite or pipestone (A stone sacred to the Native Americans of the region, primarily used to carve the bowls of ceremonial pipes.)

Don't Be Fooled by Imitations

At the 170-ft. landing, visitors descending the stairs are greeted by a carving of an obelisk many mistake for the Washington Monument. However, the stone from Charlestown, Mass., bears the likeness of another famous stone tower, the Bunker Hill Monument.

Standing on the site of the 1775 Battle of Bunker Hill, the Bunker Hill Monument was completed five years before construction on the Washington Monument began.

(For more about the Bunker Hill Monument, see Chapter Eight.)

It's All Greek
(and Latin and Chinese and Welsh) to Me

Many of the stones from foreign nations, and several from domestic donors, bear inscriptions in a foreign language. Only the Ryukyu Stone from Okinawa also carries the English translation as well. Here are translations of some of the foreign inscriptions:

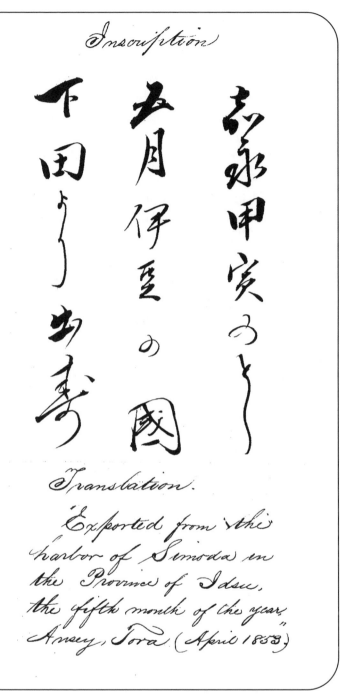

Inscription

高泉甲寅のとし
五月伊豆の國
下田より出帆

Translation.

"Exported from the harbor of Simoda in the Province of Idsu, the fifth month of the year, Ansey, Tora (April 1853.)"

A copy of the inscription on the Japanese stone and its translation, from the files of the National Archives.

✳ Hawaii (Polynesian): "The life of the land is perpetuated in righteousness." (*State motto*)

✳ New Mexico (Latin): "It grows as it goes." (*State motto*)

✳ Turkey: "So as to strengthen the friendship between the two countries, Abdul-Majid Kahn has also had his name written on the Monument to Washington" (*Abdul-Majid was the Ottoman Sultan who donated the stone.*)

✳ Bremen, Germany: "Friendly Bremen to the great, good and just Washington."

✳ Japan: "Exported from the harbor of Simoda in the Province of Isu, the fifth month of the year Ansey Tora (April, 1853)."

✳ Greece: "George Washington, the hero, the citizen of the new and illustrious liberty: the land of Solon, Themistocles and Pericles—the mother of ancient liberty—sends this ancient stone as a testimony of honor and admiration from the Parthenon."

✳ Wales: "Our language, our country, our birthplace" "Wales forever"

✳ American Medical Association (Latin): "Love of country prevails." (*The stone shows Hippocrates, the Father of Modern Medicine, refusing the riches offered him in an attempt to lure him away from Greece and into the service of the King of Persia.*)

China's Most Eloquent Tribute

Perhaps the most eloquent, and certainly the longest, tribute to Washington from a foreign source is inscribed on the stone from a missionary settlement in China. It reads in part:

"It is evident that George Washington was a remarkable man...(H)e extended the frontiers thousands of miles, and then refused to usurp the regal dignity or transmit it to his posterity, but first established rules for an elective administration....

"The United States of America regard it promotive of national virtue generally and extensively neither to establish titles of nobility and royalty nor to conform to the

⟶

> age, as respects customs and public influence, but instead deliver over their own public deliberations and inventions, so that the like of such a nation—one so remarkable—does not exist in ancient or modern times. Among the people of the Great West, can any man, in ancient or modern times, fail to pronounce Washington peerless?"

Two-fers

While one commemorative stone was good enough for most states, two states are represented in the monument twice.

In 1850, Georgia sent a marble plaque bearing the inscription "The Union as it was, Constitution as it is," a criticism of the growing powers of the federal government and the increasing influence of free-soil forces in Congress. The stone was authorized by Gov. George W.B. Towns, a staunch secessionist. That stone is mounted in the wall at the monument's 50-ft. level.

In 1852, after Towns left office, a more moderate state government under Govenor Howell Cobb sent another stone bearing the state seal and the inscription "Georgia Convention 1850." That stone can be viewed from the 240-ft. landing.

Utah's double dip is less political in nature. In 1853, Govenor Brigham Young ordered a stone bearing the likeness of a beehive sent to Washington on behalf of the settlers of the Territory of Deseret, Utah's original name. Sent before the completion of the transcontinental railroad, it took the stone three months to travel to Washington. Carried to the capital by Mormon missionaries, the stone made much of the journey in hand carts and ox-drawn wagons.

Although Utah became a state in 1896, it wasn't until 1951 that the state sent a second stone to the monument indicating that the territory had changed its name and gained statehood. The newer stone was installed directly below the Deseret stone at the 240- ft.level.

Not Desert, not Dessert, but Deseret.

When Brigham Young led his Mormon settlers to the banks of the Great Salt Lake in 1846, he named the territory Deseret, a word found in the Book of Mormon and derived from the ancient Hebrew word for honeybee. Young envisioned a community of hard-working, interdependent citizens, and found inspiration in the industrious honeybee.

Deseret Territory originally encompassed a large area of the American West, and parts of it were incorporated into what are now Idaho, Colorado, New Mexico, Arizona, California, Nevada as well as modern-day Utah. When Deseret petitioned for statehood, the territory needed to convince the federal government that the new state would have a secular government, not one controlled by the Mormon Church. As a concession to critics in Washington, the territory dropped Deseret, a name associated with the Book of Mormon, in favor of Utah, a name derived from the native peoples of the area.

Despite the name change, the honeybee symbol lives on in Utah. The state's nickname is "the Beehive State," its state motto is "Industry," and the *Deseret News* of Salt Lake City is one of the state's leading newspapers.

Siam, I Am

A dark brown stone on the monument's 190-ft. level bears a single word, "SIAM." Some youngsters, misreading the word as "slam," have expressed the notion that the stone may have been donated by Michael Jordan, but that is not the case.

The stone's donor was actually the Second King of Siam, King Chululongkorn, also known as Rama IV. His father, King Mongkut (Rama III), opened Siam to the West and was portrayed in the Rogers and Hammerstein musical "The King and I."

As a young prince, Chululongkorn studied Western civilization and became enamored with American democracy in general and George Washington in particular. He was such an admirer of Washington that he took for himself the title "Prince George Washington" and insisted on being addressed by that title. During his reign, King Rama IV continued his father's modernization policies and managed to maintain independence as nearby territories were being taken as colonies by imperial European powers, most significantly Britain and France.

In the modern era, the Kingdom of Siam is known as Thailand.

Odd Fellows and Masons and Redmen! Oh, My!

George Washington held high rank in the Masonic Order, so Masonic lodges throughout the country were more than eager to honor one of their own with memorial stones donated to the Washington Monument. Some 20 of the 194 memorial stones in the staircase were donated by Masonic organizations.

Other lodges and fraternal societies are also represented. They include the Independent Order of Odd Fellows, Sons of Temperance, Improved Order of Redmen, and the Hibernian Society.

Saving Private Hasam

At the monument's 270-ft. level is a large stone of white variegated marble donated by the Continental Guard of New Orleans, a local militia. The stone is 6 ft., 8 in. wide and 4 ft., 3 in. high, making it one of the largest stones in the collection.

The Continental Guard stone is inscribed with the names of the men who served in the organization at the time the stone was donated. For observers uninterested in these names, the stone bears little else of note, until the reader's eye reaches the final column of names and notices something unusual. One of the names, Thomas Hasam, is carved in a recess in the face of the stone. Most likely the stone carver made an error, perhaps misspelled Hasam's name. With the inscription of the names almost complete, the carver would not have wanted to grind down the entire face of the stone and start over, so he ground down only the name with the error, Hasam's, and carved in the correction.

A stone from the Grand Lodge of Iowa, Ancient Free and Accepted Masons, is one of more than 20 stones donated to the monument by Masonic organizations to honor brother Mason George Washington.

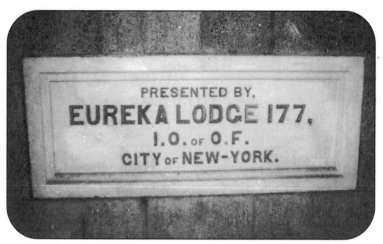

The Independent Order of Odd Fellows is one of several fraternal organizations represented in the monument's collection of memorial stones.

It is safe to assume that Thomas Hasam was not pleased with the carver's error, or his correction, which left Hasam's name at the bottom of a recess in the stone. Still, Hasam had the last laugh. On a stone with a face of more than 25 square feet, containing the names of the Governor and Lt. Governor of Louisiana, and the commanding general, officer corps and entire membership of the militia, the name of Pvt. Thomas Hasam, recessed because of a stone carver's error, stands out. In fact, of all the names on that stone, Pvt. Hasam's is the only one mentioned in this book.

The Bard of the Potomac?

Many of the memorial stones, not surprisingly, bear images of the man they are designed to honor, George Washington. However, Washington is not the only famous person depicted on the commemorative stones. The face of another President, Thomas Jefferson, is carved on a stone from the Jefferson Medical College of Philadelphia. Jefferson's representation in the monument is not surprising. He was a contemporary of Washington's, and a great statesman in his own right.

Not one, but two memorial stones bear the likeness of another historic figure. He was long dead by Washington's time. He was not even an American. The man is English playwright William Shakespeare (1564-1616). Shakespeare's face adorns a stone donated by the Thalian Association of Wilmington, North Carolina, and another stone given by the "Ladies and Gentlemen of the Dramatic Profession of America."

This second stone bears an interesting inscription, "All That Live Must Die." The quote is from Shakespeare's play "Hamlet." The stone makes no reference to Washington, his ideals or his accomplishments. The quote, selected from all of the wonderful words penned by Shakespeare, is downright depressing. Nothing in the monument's records indicates why this quote was carved in the stone.

Could it be that the stone was ordered by an actor who had just missed out on an important role?

*The Oklahoma stone displays the state seal. The star at the center
of the seal celebrates the state's Native American heritage. It represents
the Five Civilized Tribes which were relocated by the U.S. government
in the 19th Century from the East Coast to the territory that is
now the state of Oklahoma.*

*The Sons of Temperance, a group dedicated to the elimination
of alcohol consumption, is one of the fraternal societies represented
in the monument. The Sons of Temperance of Rhode Island
is one of the state chapters to send a stone.*

Onward and Upward! (Just Not Yet!)

The State of New York's official stone holds a prominent place at the 160-ft. level. The dark granite stone displays the state coat of arms and the state motto: "Excelsior."

Roughly translated from the Latin, "Excelsior" means "Onward and upward!" Ironically, the stone is located just above a bench where weary climbers could take a break.

Perhaps the New York stone and its motto were placed there for encouragement.

Local Folks

The three local jurisdictions in the National Capital area are represented at the Washington Monument's 90-foot level, where stones from the State of Virginia, the City of Washington, D.C., and the State of Maryland are on display.

The stone from the City of Washington is positioned between the stones from Maryland and Virginia, which is appropriate since the District of Columbia was carved from territory that once belonged to the two states.

As the District of Columbia Shrank, Washington, D.C. Grew

When Congress selected a site for the permanent seat of the federal government, it chose a 100-square-mile diamond of land straddling the Potomac River. About 70 percent of the territory for the new federal district, the District of Columbia, was carved from Maryland and the rest from Virginia.

The district included the new capital city, Washington, but also incorporated two cities that had existed on the site before the arrival of the federal government. The cities of Alexandria, Virginia, and Georgetown, Maryland, became Alexandria, D.C. and Georgetown, D.C.

———➤

In 1846, Congress decided to return the portion of the district south of the river to Virginia. This included the city of Alexandria and what is now Arlington County. The area now includes the Pentagon, Reagan National Airport, Arlington National Cemetery, and a population of more than 300,000.

Across the river, the city of Washington grew steadily. What began as a cluster of government buildings between Capitol Hill and Foggy Bottom soon began to encroach on neighboring Georgetown. In 1871, Washington absorbed its neighbor, and Georgetown, D.C., ceased to exist as a separate city. Modern day Washington encompasses the entire territory of the District of Columbia.

Some Georgetown residents and businesses, however, still cling to the one-time independence of their neighborhood, and stubbornly use the address "Georgetown, D.C."

Chapter Four

Ups and Downs

When the Washington Monument opened to the public in 1888, it was the tallest building in the world, standing taller than the great cathedrals of Europe and the great pyramids of Egypt. Visitors never before had enjoyed the opportunity to climb so high into the sky and observe the world from 500 feet above the ground. Riding the building's elevator was also a new experience in itself.

However, over the years, some visitors managed to find novel ways to go up and down the monument.

"Where Women Faint and Strong Men Tremble"

Although the Washington Monument was dedicated in 1885, it took three years to open the monument to the public. One reason for the delay was the refitting of the steam-powered hoist that had been used to haul blocks of granite and marble to the upper reaches of the tower into an elevator suitable for carrying visitors to the 500-ft. observation deck.

When the monument and its elevator opened to the public in 1888, the *Washington Star* of the day referred to the elevator as the place "where women faint and strong men tremble." Although the ride was perfectly safe (the hoist machinery was designed to carry 10 tons of stone), travel to such heights by way of a steel cable was new and frightening to many visitors of the day.

The elevator car was partially enclosed with corrugated metal, but had openings sufficient to allow passengers to observe the memorial stones lining the stairway walls. The ascent took about 12 minutes, the descent 10. The elevator made one round trip every half hour.

Newer, faster elevators reduced these times. The current

elevator, installed in 2002, takes about 70 sec. to climb to the top, making round trips every five minutes.

The faster elevators, however, did not stop some of the visitors from fainting. Monument personnel still had to deal with three or four such incidents a day. Then the Park Service installed a recording to tell visitors the story of the monument as they ascended the 500 feet to the top of the tower. The recording apparently took elevator occupants' minds off the fact that the ground was quickly dropping beneath their feet and kept them distracted until the elevator car reached the observation level. After the debut of the recording, fainting incidents dropped to three or four a year.

Today, rangers have taken the place of the recorded speech and provide information about the monument during the elevator ride.

Women and Children...Not!

A popular myth about the early days of the monument's elevator goes something like this: "The first elevator was an open platform suspended by a cable. It would sway back and forth as it rose to the top of the monument. For this reason, it was deemed unsafe for women and children, so only men were allowed to ride it. The men, knowing they had a 12-minute ride ahead of them, would pass the time with fruit, brandy and cigars while their wives and children climbed the stairs."

This story is very popular with local tour guides. A variation of the myth claims women were not allowed on the elevator because champagne was served on board and it was unseemly for ladies to be where alcohol was served.

Research has turned up no such prohibition on women or children from the elevator. Women were aboard when the monument and the refitted elevator were opened in 1888. Instead of an open, free swinging platform, visitors were carried to the top in a car with metal walls and roof. Rails and guides were employed to eliminate sway, and safety systems were installed to keep the elevator from falling if the cable broke.

There is also no record of champagne, brandy or refreshments of any kind being served or consumed routinely on the monument's elevator. Furthermore, in its early years the monument was run by the

"Where women faint and strong men tremble."
The monument's first elevator provided a new experience to
visitors. Despite some popular myths to the contrary, women have
always been allowed to ride the elevator since the monument
opened to the public in 1888.

Army, and it is unlikely that the Army would permit the consumption of alcohol on the elevator.

There is the possibility that special tours for visiting dignitaries could have involved champagne or other refreshments. These also could have been men-only events. However, as a general rule, women and children have always been welcome on the elevator since the monument opened to the general public.

The Monument Dash

No official records have been kept of the fastest time up and down the monument's steps. However, a likely contender for the record would be Jerry Zettle, a helper on the crew installing the new elevator in 1959. It was Zettle's job to ferry parts and tools from ground level to workers at the top of the monument. Zettle, 23, could make the round trip in 18 minutes: 11 up, seven down, which was faster in both directions than the original elevator.

Age is Just a Number

Similarly, no official records have been kept on the oldest person to climb the monument's staircase, nor is there an official mark for the most climbs. One octogenarian who could challenge for both titles is Gustav Hergert. On December 11, 1965, the *Washington Daily News* reported that Hergert, 75, climbed the steps for the 1,000th time. He made the climb in 18 minutes flat.

Six years later, on January 15, 1972, the *Washington Star* covered Hergert's 2,000th trip up the monument stairs. The 81-year-old Hergert's climbing time on this date was not reported.

No record holder, but still worth mention, is George Frederick Miller. On May 10, 1950, Miller climbed the 898 steps to celebrate his 70th birthday. The *Washington Times-Herald* reported that Miller rode his bicycle six miles from his home to the monument before his climb that morning, and pedaled home afterward.

And one feisty lady was prevented from attempting to set a record that would have been hard to break. In 1948, Georgia Ireland, age 98, was stopped from trying to climb the monument staircase by her two sons, both of whom were Washington, D.C., police officers.

The monument's staircase at the 160-ft. level.
Several landings along the stairway include benches for weary
climbers. The monument's stairs were closed in 1976 except
for guided tours.

Mrs. Ireland told reporters she had wanted to climb the monument's steps since the building opened, 60 years before.

Unusual Ascents and Descents

Over the years, some visitors have chosen unconventional ways to traverse the monument steps:

*   In 1933, a man named Paul Conrad climbed the monument's 898 steps carrying a 145-pound man, according to Ripley's *Believe It or Not*. The climb took 16$^1/_2$ minutes, and was completed with no stops along the way.

*   In 1950, an acrobat (identified by one newspaper as Glenn Marlin and another as Glenn Sinby) descended the 898 steps on his hands. It took one hour, 25 minutes.

*   Also in 1950, another acrobat, Russell Nesbit, tried to break the record for hand-walking down the monument stairs. Accompanied by a 13-year-old assistant, Nesbit got about 165 feet down the stairs when the elevator operator stopped the elevator, got out and chased Nesbit back up the steps. When the elevator resumed its descent, Nesbit resumed his attempt to break the record. Before he could get much farther, however, he was met on the steps by Superintendent John H. Bushong, who put an end to the stunt. Bushong said if he allowed such stunts to continue, people would keep coming back with more and more outrageous ideas. "Others might be encouraged to roll down the steps on their stomachs," he said.

*   Herbert J. Blitz, a clerk at the Department of Commerce, climbed the staircase on crutches on March 2, 1958. "I can climb as many stairs as anyone," Blitz told the *Washington Post*, "only I'm slower." The climb took Blitz one hour and 20 minutes. Blitz also traversed the stairs backwards. "It's easier to climb facing down," he said. Blitz, 29, had broken his back seven years earlier and could not walk without the aid of his crutches.

*   On December 21, 1961, the *Washington Post* reported that Jonathan Dickey made the climb on stilts. Dickey's feat came to light when he auditioned for the television show "Ted Mack's Original Amateur Hour," in hopes of winning the chance to show his skill with stilts on TV. Dickey, a helper on a newspaper delivery truck, said he trained for his monument climb by going up and down the steps in his house over and over again.

✳ Six high school boys in March, 1963, staged a piggy-back race up the monument stairs. The winning team made the climb in 15 minutes, 30 seconds. They attributed their victory to the strategy of changing places at each landing. Although they said they were too tired to plant their school banner at the top of the monument, the six boys from Annandale, VA., raced back down the monument staircase, individually this time, reaching the base of the monument in five minutes flat.

✳ A *Washington Post* item in June, 1963 reported that three girls from Chevy Chase, Md., claimed to be the first three-girl American team to climb the Washington Monument stairway backwards.

Tapped Out

In October, 1993, dancer Carol Vaughn tap danced her way down the monument's staircase. (Eat your heart out, Fred Astaire!) Vaughn said the Park Service denied her permission to dance down the stairway as a charity fundraiser, so she did it on the sly.

"I told them I wasn't going to be dancing. More like artistic walking," Vaughn said.

Vaughn said she and an accomplice joined a tour to gain access to the staircase, but hung back from the rest of the group until the tour was well down the stairway. Vaughn then tapped her way to the bottom nonstop.

The Park Service had been tipped off that Vaughn was planning to do the stunt and had Park Police standing by when she reached the bottom of the steps. However, Vaughn saw the police before they saw her. She ducked back into the monument, removed her tap shoes, and blended in with a crowd of tourists, giving the authorities the slip.

One More Time!

How many times in a row can a 65-year-old man climb an 898-step staircase? Howard Hardaway, 65, of Louisville, Ky., wanted to find out. On May 13, 1964, Hardaway came to the monument to climb the stairway over and over again until he had his answer. Hardaway entered the monument at 4:05 p.m. that day, and completed his first round trip at 4:30. Hardaway made five more round trips of the monument stairs that day. Each trip took about 25 minutes, and he rested only five minutes or so between climbs. He completed his sixth and final round trip at 6:54 p.m. Hardaway said he made the climbs to settle a bet.

And the Man Jumped over the Monument

David G. Morris of Olney, Md., claimed to have jumped over the Washington Monument.

His 1962 obituary in the *Washington Star* reported that Morris performed the feat "in the1930's." (Most likely it was 1934.) At the time, Morris was friends with the engineer in charge of the repairs that were underway at the monument. The building was surrounded by scaffolding and the engineer invited Morris to come visit the top of the monument. Morris posed for photographs on the platform at the tip of the monument. The top three feet or so of the structure poked through the floor of the platform. In one shot, Morris posed like he was using the tip as a golf tee. Then, he had an idea. He jumped over the exposed apex, landing safely on the enclosed platform on the other side, and winning the distinction of having jumped over the Washington Monument.

Morris said when he told his young son what he did, "He didn't doubt me, but he couldn't figure out how I did it."

Hold onto Your Skirts!

Also in 1934, a female employee of the Department of Labor made an unexpected trip to the very tip of the monument

As part of her job, Blanche Wilcox of Washington had been sending workers to the monument to help with the cleaning and repairs underway at the time. One day, she decided to go to the monument herself and check on these workers.

When she got there, the foreman in charge of the project challenged her to ride the rickety construction lift up the exterior scaffolding to the top of the structure. To the foreman's surprise, Wilcox accepted. Not only did she ride the lift, she climbed the rope ladder the last 50 feet to the tip. She made the climb despite wearing a long skirt, which she had to control in the wind.

When she recounted the story for the *Washington Daily News* 30 years later, she said she would change only one thing about her experience: She'd wear pants.

"If I only had stretchpants," Wilcox told the paper, "I'd climb it again tomorrow."

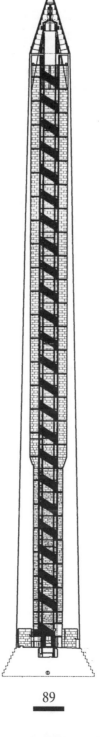

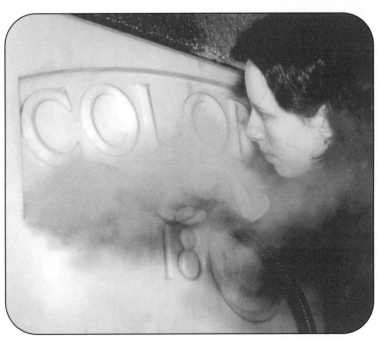

JUDITH M. JACOB, NATIONAL PARK SERVICE, NORTHEAST CULTURAL RESOURCES CENTER

Naomi Kroll, a conservator from the National Park Service's Northeast Cultural Resources Center, cleans the face of the Colorado stone during the 1996-2000 renovations. Over the years, workers have had to clean fingerprints, chewing gum, even lipstick from the memorial stones. Vandalism has been a problem since the monument's early days.

Chapter Five:

Vandals!

In 1971, because of an increasing number of health problems experienced by visitors trying to climb the stairs to the observation level, the National Park Service closed the stairs to people going up. Everyone had to take the elevator to the top, but, once there, visitors could choose to walk down the stairs.

In 1976 the Park Service closed the main stairway to the general public altogether because of the growing incidence of vandalism, littering and horseplay on the stairs. Lacking the staff to constantly patrol the 50-story staircase, the Park Service required all visitors to take the elevator up and back, and limited access to the stairway and the commemorative stones to group tours led by a ranger or trained volunteer

Vandalism, however, is not a modern phenomenon. The earliest days of the monument saw damage from graffiti artists and souvenir hunters of the time.

"Bad Chirography"

Less than four months after the monument opened to the public, vandalism had become an evident and growing problem. In his report to the Monument Commission on February 9, 1889, the monument's superintendent told of damage to the memorial stones, including the removal of brass lettering from the Switzerland stone, words cut into the monument's walls and damage to figures carved on some of the stones.

In reporting on the vandalism, the *Washington Evening Star* wrote, "Names of persons not entitled to fame have been scrawled to bad chirography on prominent places; bits of excruciating rhyme are to be found here and there; sentiments sometimes of a doubtful character defile the walls until the monument has come to be a veritable book on stone, and not a very high order of literature at that."

The Family Fallon

Even before the Washington Monument was open to the public, graffitists were at work.

At the 90-ft. level, between the bottom row of commemorative stones and the staircase landing, is scrawled "L+ Fallon, 1879." A few levels above is another inscription, in the first row of blocks above the landing and therefore less obvious. It reads simply, "W. FAL." There may have been more to this second inscription, but the block next to it is heavily damaged and no more letters are visible.

These inscriptions may be the work of members of the Fallon family.

William Fallon Sr. and his wife, Ellen, were born in Ireland and were probably among the thousands of Irish immigrants who came to the United States to escape the Potato Famine. By1857, the couple had settled in Maryland, where their first child, Anne, was born. Their migrating days were not over, however. During the next two decades, the Fallon family made its home in Ohio, Washington, D.C., Virginia, and Pennsylvania, adding five sons and three more daughters along the way. The family eventually returned to the District of Columbia and settled into a home on I St. NW.

According to the Washington Monument's payroll records, William Fallon, Sr. was hired as a laborer in November of 1878. In 1879, he was joined on the job by sons Lawrence, age 20, John, 19, and William, Jr., 16.

Lawrence Fallon is probably responsible for the "L+ Fallon 1879" inscription and "W. FAL" was probably William, Sr. Both Lawrence and his father were listed on the payroll as skilled laborers, while the other Fallons were listed as common laborers. This distinction may have given William Sr. and Lawrence more access to the monument's interior and more opportunity to carve their names in its walls. The "+" in Lawrence's carving may be his way of including the other Fallons in the inscription, or simply a substitute for a period in the abbreviation of his name.

John Fallon left his job at the monument in May, 1880. William Sr. left in July and William Jr. and Lawrence worked through September. The records do not indicate if they quit, or were discharged.

Profound Vandalism

It is ironic that fresh graffiti is considered vandalism, while 100-year-old graffiti is treated as an historical artifact.

Such is the case with an inscription uncovered during a 1994 renovation of the elevator waiting area at the monument's base. When workers removed a section of marble wainscoting in a rear alcove, they found an inscription that had been covered for more than 100 years. It reads:

"Whoever is the human instrument under God in the convertion [sic] of one soul, erects a monument to his own memory loftier, and more enuring [sic] than this."

The initials B.F.B. accompany this profound bit of graffiti. The second "B" may not have been part of the original inscription. It is carved with single strokes, not retraced several times like the rest of the letters in the message. Either the carver was interrupted before he could go over the last letter again, or someone added the final B at a later time. No one knows who B.F.,or B.F.B., was. (Benjamin Franklin it was not; Franklin was long dead by the time the monument's construction began.) Could it have been William (Bill) Fallon, Sr. or Jr.? We will probably never know.

A Victim of Human Nature and Mother Nature

Not all of the damage done to the memorial stones is the work of vandals. Many of the stones in the monument have been damaged by the weather. Even though the stones are installed inside the monument, they have been affected by temperature, precipitation, and humidity.

Some stones, especially those carved from softer materials, have been damaged by erosion. During times of heavy rain, leaks in the monument's stonework allowed water to run down the interior walls.

Over the years, this "indoor rain" washed smooth many of the distinct edges of figures carved in these softer stones.

Even stones carved from sturdier material are not immune to the effects of this phenomenon. Winters in Washington, D.C., are very damp and rainy. Often, temperatures will rise above freezing during the day and drop below the freezing point at night. During such weather, water running down the interior walls would penetrate into tiny cracks or flaws in the memorial stones. At night, when the temperature dropped, the water froze and expanded, enlarging the crack. During the warmer temperatures of the day, the ice thawed and the water ran deeper into the enlarged crack, repeating the freeze-thaw cycle until the moisture eventually evaporated.

A stone at the 90-ft. level, donated by the Mechanics of Raleigh, North Carolina, is most likely the victim of the weather. However, Mother Nature did not act alone. She had help from human nature.

The Mechanics' stone is located at the top of the flight of stairs rising from the 80-ft. level to the 90-ft. level. It is likely that, in the days when visitors were allowed to climb the stairs to the observation deck, long lines of tourists, probably hot, tired, and a bit bored after climbing nine flights and realizing that there were 41 more to go, found this weather-damaged stone an easy target for mischief. A chip here, a flake there, initials carved here and there, and the face of the stone was slowly etched away.

A sign above the stone now tells visitors what was originally engraved on the stone, because the message that once read "From the Mechanics of Raleigh, N.C.," now reads only "F."

Mr. Washington's Dirty Nose

As visitors climbed the monument's stairway over the years, an informal tradition took hold. People began rubbing the noses of the carved figures with their fingers, perhaps for luck, more likely for lack of anything more interesting to do during the climb.

Despite the benign nature of this act, the oily residue deposited on the statuary by the tourists' fingertips accumulated over the years to mar the appearance of several of the memorial stones. One of the stones most affected by this tradition is the State of Washington stone. Located at the 310-ft. level, the block bears a relief of the state seal, the main feature of which is a portrait of George Washington. As visitors practiced the traditional nose rubbing on the Washington stone, the porous red sandstone absorbed body oil, dirt and perspiration from the rubbing fingers. These deposits darkened the color of the stone, giving Washington's face a black nose and prompting still other tourists to rub the nose in an attempt to remove the dark substance, only to make the condition worse.

Washington's dirty nose stayed that way until 1999, when the stone was cleaned as part of the overall renovation of the monument. With access to the memorial stones restricted to supervised tours, it is easier now for Mr. Washington to keep his nose clean.

Lady Baltimore's Missing Head

At the 140-ft. landing is one of the largest memorial stones in the monument, donated by the City of Baltimore, Md. Six feet high and six feet wide, the stone displays a relief carving of the Baltimore Battle Monument. The monument stands in the intersection of Pratt and Gay Streets in downtown Baltimore. It commemorates the bombardment of Fort McHenry during the War of 1812, the battle that saved Baltimore from invasion and inspired our national anthem.

The Battle Monument shows an allegorical female figure, dubbed "Lady Baltimore" by the locals, standing atop a tall pillar mounted on a pedestal. It was dedicated in 1825 and its image is even incorporated into Baltimore's official city seal.

This reverence for the monument and the battle it commemorates mattered little to an intrepid vandal viewing the Baltimore stone inside the Washington Monument. Using cracks and ledges in the monument wall, and maybe a boost from an accomplice, the clever criminal scaled to a height more than ten feet from the landing floor to snatch the head off the shoulders of Lady Baltimore.

This act of vandalism was corrected in the 1999 renovations.

The Flag Was Still There

In early August, 1814, the British invaded Washington, D.C., and burned the Capitol, White House and other government buildings. The invaders then turned their attention to Baltimore. The city's harbor was home port to many American privateers, armed merchant ships licensed to raid enemy shipping. The Royal Navy wanted to wipe out what they considered "a nest of pirates."

In order to enter Baltimore Harbor, however, the fleet had to pass by the American shore defenses, the most formidable of which was Fort McHenry. The fort's commander, Lt. Col. George Armistead, expecting a British attack, ordered an oversized flag—30 by 42 feet—to be flown above the fort as an act of defiance.

On September 13, 1814, the British fleet began its siege of Ft. McHenry. Firing bombs and rockets, the warships continued their attack for 25 hours. The defenses held, however, and the British withdrew.

A young American attorney who had witnessed the battle, Francis Scott Key, wrote a poem inspired by what he saw. His poem began, "O, say can you see, by the dawn's early light, what so proudly we hailed at the twilight's last gleaming?" Key's poem, "The Star Spangled Banner," was later put to music and, in 1931, Congress made the song our national anthem. The flag that inspired Key is now in the Smithsonian Institution's National Museum of American History, two blocks east of the Washington Monument.

Take Home a Piece of the Rock?

When you visit the Washington Monument, look closely at the corners of the building. The marble stonework at all four corners has been replaced from ground level to about as high as a person can reach. The work was done to repair damage done by over-eager visitors in search of a souvenir.

During the early history of the monument, Washington, D.C., did not have the souvenir shops, book stores and t-shirt stands that now pepper the Mall area and downtown, so visitors had to use their own ingenuity to find a fitting memento. Some visitors thought a chunk of marble from the Washington Monument would make a dandy souvenir, so they would chip a piece off the corner of the tower to show Mom and the kids back home.

Today, anyone in search of a souvenir is directed to the gift shop.

Leave it to Beaver

A popular parable about George Washington tells how the Founding Father, as a young boy, confessed to cutting down the family's cherry tree. However, George cannot be blamed for the chopping—more accurately, chomping—that took place in the shadow of his monument in 1999.

Just south of the Washington Monument grounds is a man-made lake known as the Tidal Basin. Every spring, the park surrounding the Tidal Basin is awash in pink and white as thousands of Japanese cherry trees burst into flower. Cherry blossom time in Washington, D.C. is one of the most popular times to visit the capital city.

In early April, 1999, as the cherry blossoms were at their peak, visitors and locals alike were shocked to find out that a band of vandals was cutting down these beloved trees under cover of night. They chose their targets carefully, and before they were done, they had taken down four of the precious cherry trees and six other trees on park property

The National Park Service set a trap for the vandals, and within a few days had them all in custody. The perpetrators, a family of beavers, were removed to another pond in the city, far away from the famous cherry trees.

A Sticky Situation

In the days when the public was allowed free access to the monument's staircase, cleaners faced a sticky challenge: dealing with the chewing gum that appeared everywhere.

When the monument closed for its annual cleaning, crews used putty knives to scrape the dried goo off the stairs, the landings, the walls, the memorial stones and elsewhere. The offending gum was hauled out of the monument by the bucketful.

Chewing gum was not the most difficult substance to remove from the staircase and memorial stones. According to newspaper accounts, the cleaning crews' toughest challenge was removing the names, initials and other messages written on the walls in red lipstick. Cleaners had to use acid to remove them.

Love Notes

In an effort to protect the walls near the windows at the observation level from additional graffiti, the National Park Service in 1976 installed plexiglass covers over the marble. The new covering protected the walls from further destruction from visitors writing or scratching messages there, but opened the door to a new form of vandalism.

Ten years later, a visitor undaunted by the plexiglass slipped a note behind the transparent cover. Other notes and messages followed. So did business cards, advertisements, postcards, even blank checks. As the messages mounted, the Park Service was forced to remove the covering to clear out the trash that had accumulated behind.

Spiderman?

The most daring act of vandalism at the monument was the theft that occurred in December of 1934. With the monument surrounded by scaffolding for repairs, a thief climbed to the very top of the scaffold and stole 107 small lightning rods from the monument's tip. The rods, each tipped with gold or platinum, were valued at $8.00 apiece, or $856 total, no small sum in 1934.

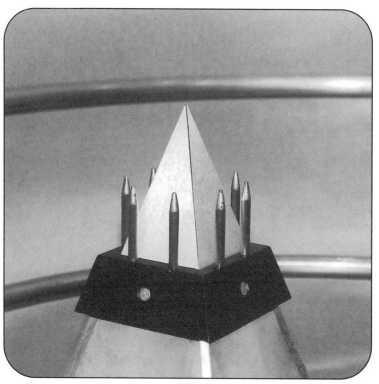

J. BERARD

A National Park Service exhibit includes a mock-up of the monument's capstone, including replicas of the aluminum tip and some of the lightning suppressors. In 1934 a thief made off with 107 of the small lightning rods, valued at $856.

J. BERARD

*A sign similar to this one was the only casualty when
an Indiana man fired two blasts from a shotgun on the monument
grounds in 1997.*

Chapter 6

The Dark Side of the Monument

The Washington Monument's construction was completed without a major accident or the loss of life. That was certainly a phenomenal accomplishment when you consider that the workers were building a stone tower to a height no one had reached before, and were doing it without today's sophisticated technology and safety requirements.

Yet, there are dark spots on the monument's history. Four people have taken their own lives by jumping from the tower's open windows or down the elevator shaft. A fifth death was accidental. The most recent such event occurred in 1949. (The windows are now kept closed and locked; the elevator shaft is separated from the stairs by a 6 foot-high fence and access to the stairway is restricted.)

Such a prominent landmark will often draw the attention of those who would use it to make a personal or political statement, often without regard to the lives and safety of innocent people who may be in the area at the time, and the forces of nature are always unpredictable. This chapter recounts some of these darker incidents at the Washington Monument.

Spy Catcher

In the years following World War II, a tense rivalry developed between the United States and the Soviet Union. Both made use of the intelligence networks developed during the war to keep a watch on each other and gather whatever information they could in order to gain an edge over the other.

A *Parade* magazine article by Jack Anderson and Fred Blumenthal on January 6, 1957, told the story of one Cold War spy who was caught red-handed at the Washington Monument.

In the late 1940s and early '50s, a Soviet spy ring operating in Vienna, Austria, tried to collect military secrets from American servicemen. It would try to pick out officers and enlisted men who could be bribed or blackmailed into providing information. The ring would ask for simple things at first, such as a telephone directory, then press for more sensitive documents.

In 1949, the Soviet agents approached a U.S. Air Force officer, identified in the story only as Major X, and recruited him as one of their informants. What the agents did not know at the time was that Major X was actually a counterintelligence officer, a spy catcher.

Major X played along with the agents, giving them documents carefully doctored to give them false information without arousing suspicion.

Two years later, the scene shifted to Washington, D.C. The Vienna spy ring took its direction from an agent at the Soviet Embassy in Washington. After two years of playing along, Major X had worked his way into the group's confidence. The Soviets wanted information on U.S. military installations in Europe, and they wanted Major X to deliver it directly to one of their diplomats in Washington.

The *Parade* article describes how a meeting was set up between the two men in April, 1951. Major X was to show up at the Washington Monument at the appointed time. He was told to wear a snap-brim hat pulled low over his eyes, carry a newspaper under his arm and hold his right glove in his left hand. He followed the instructions and the trap was set.

Major X was approached by Yuri Norikov, the Soviet diplomat. The major handed the Soviet a packet of information, doctored in order to protect U.S. security. Meanwhile, FBI agents were stationed a short distance away and caught the exchange on film.

The counterspy agents did not swoop in and arrest Norikov. Instead, they allowed the spy ring to continue to operate for two more years. All the while, American agents were spying on the spies, learning their methods and their contacts and continuing to feed them false information through Major X.

Finally, in 1953, U.S. agents busted the ring. Norikov, protected from arrest by diplomatic immunity, was expelled from the United States. The Cold War continued for another 40 years, but the Americans had won this round of spy vs. counterspy.

Bomb Plot Foiled

On February 17, 1965, Washington newspapers reported that the previous day federal agents in New York had arrested four people suspected in a plot to blow up the Washington Monument and other national landmarks. Three men and one woman were taken into custody and 20 sticks of dynamite were recovered. One of those arrested reportedly smuggled the dynamite into the country from Canada. The group was described in the *Washington Post* as "pro-Castro, pro-China."

Besides the Washington Monument, the group had reportedly also targeted the Statue of Liberty in New York Harbor and the Liberty Bell in Philadelphia.

Standoff

The most spectacular of these dark incidents took place on December 8, 1982. On that morning, a peace activist named Norman Mayer drove a van to the monument's entrance, claimed to have 1,000 pounds of TNT, and threatened to detonate the explosives if the country did not take steps to eliminate nuclear weapons.

Experts said even a half ton of TNT would not be enough to penetrate the monument's 15-foot-thick stone walls and bring the building down. Police, however, feared people could be hurt by flying debris if such a bomb were detonated. They also feared the explosion would shatter windows in nearby buildings, and endanger those inside from flying glass.

Police secured the area and civilians were evacuated from the monument grounds. Seven museums and eight nearby government office buildings were closed and some 20,000 federal workers were sent home. At the White House, five blocks north, President Ronald Reagan's scheduled luncheon was moved to a room away from windows facing the monument. First Lady Nancy Reagan and White House staff were also cautioned to stay away from the side of the building facing the monument.

Mayer told police he would only talk to a representative of the news media, and he called upon the Washington press corps to delegate one of their members—one with no dependents—to act as an intermediary. An Associated Press reporter named Steve Kamerow volunteered. Kamerow relayed Mayer's message to authorities. According to Kamerow's account, Mayer issued rambling demands to ban nuclear weapons "or face doomsday." Kamerow also said Mayer told him he chose the Washington Monument for this action because "it's one of the sacred icons and it's accessible."

At 7:30 p.m., after a 10-hour standoff, Mayer tried to escape the police cordon and backed his van away from the monument. Police, fearing the truck could become a "moving time bomb" on the streets of Washington, opened fire. The truck traveled about 50 yards toward the northeast corner of the monument grounds through a hail of police gunfire, and overturned.

Explosives experts approached the van first and found Mayer inside, with bullet wounds to his arm, face and head. The head wound proved to be mortal and Mayer died about 90 minutes later at a local hospital. Police later said they did not intend to kill Mayer, and that they were shooting to stop the truck by disabling the engine or deflating the tires. (At least one of the rounds struck the monument itself, leaving a pock mark on the east wall, to the right of the entrance.) No explosives were found inside Mayer's truck

Police then fired tear gas into the monument building, fearing that Mayer may have had a confederate inside, but he had acted alone.

Mayer was known to many in Washington for his anti-war activism. In its story on Mayer's background, the *Washington Post* quoted a 21-year-old staffer for the Arms Control Association who had often seen Mayer handing out leaflets in the Dupont Circle area. Ten years later, that staffer, George Stephanopoulos, would be a national figure as White House Communications Director under President Bill Clinton.

Mayer's story ended in irony and controversy. Because Mayer was a disabled Navy veteran, his family insisted that he be buried at Arlington National Cemetery. Despite the circumstances of his death, and protests from veterans groups and other outraged Americans, there were no legal grounds to deny the request. So, on December 15, 1982, without military honors, Mayer's body was cremated and his ashes inurned at the cemetery's columbarium.

Accidental Hostages

As Norman Mayer held off police outside the monument, eight people—six tourists, one park ranger and the manager of the book store—were trapped inside. About the time the siege began, a ranger who was operating the elevator stepped off and accidentally let the elevator doors close behind him. A group of tourists had been waiting to ride the elevator back down to the ground floor, but the ranger was unable to reopen the elevator doors, so he escorted the tourists down the monument's staircase. Because the elevator was now inoperable, the bookstore manager closed his shop and another ranger, Tracey Williams, advised the six remaining visitors that they would also have to leave via the stairway. They followed a few minutes behind the first group.

When they reached the ground, Ranger Williams preceded the group out the stairway exit and encountered Mayer, dressed menacingly in a blue jumpsuit and dark motorcycle helmet. Mayer shouted, "Get out of here!" and Williams returned to the group, telling them they had to climb back to the top of the monument. They did.

The eight accidental hostages did not know what was happening on the ground 500 feet below them until a telephone hookup was established with the ranger station at the Survey Lodge on the monument grounds.

Finally, about 2:00 p.m., after being trapped in the building for five hours, the group was told they would be allowed to leave. They walked back down the stairs and another ranger met them about half-way to escort them. When the group reached ground level, they were able to leave one-by-one and make their way down the hill to 15th Street. Police asked each of them for a statement about the experience, then they were allowed to leave.

Speaking to reporters later, members of the group recounted the ordeal. When asked what the eight talked about while they were trapped for so many hours in the monument's observation deck, Gordon Frost, a 28-year-old carpenter from Sacramento, Calif., said, "we talked about the view."

Attack of the 18-Wheeler

A truck driver, possibly suffering side-effects from pain medication, crashed his big rig into the Washington Monument on November 20, 1985.

Garrow E. Brigham, 37, of Laurel, Md., veered his truck off Constitution Avenue and up the monument hill, crashing through a snow fence and the ring of benches and smashing into the stone tower.

According to the *Washington Post* account, a park employee approached the truck and Brigham handed him a pair of scissors and a photograph of a diamond ring.

"I want those in my office in five minutes," Brigham told the employee. When asked just where his office was, Brigham pointed to the top of the monument.

At his trial the following March, it was explained that the driver had been suffering from mental stress and possible side effects of medication he was taking for an elbow injury. Brigham pleaded guilty to destruction of government property. As part of the plea bargain, the driver agreed to pay $3,500 restitution for damage he did to the monument and grounds.

The incident occurred before the monument opened for the day. There were no injuries. The truck left some scratches on the monument, but did no structural damage. The monument opened three hours late that day because of the crash.

Shotgun Blast

An Indiana man fired two shotgun blasts on the monument grounds on October 7, 1997. According to reports, Lynn G. Thacker, 60, of Bedford, Ind., fired two blasts from a 12-gauge shotgun in the monument's parking lot off Constitution Avenue. No one was injured by the gunfire, but a metal visitor information sign was hit and damaged.

When police arrived, according to news accounts, Thacker was waiting calmly, his shotgun on the hood of his pickup truck. Thacker was arrested and charged with destruction of government property. His reasons for firing the blasts are not known.

Chapter 7:

Presidents and Celebrities and Just Plain Folks

Millions of people from all over the world have visited the Washington Monument since it was opened to the public in 1888. These have included one President, numerous celebrities, and millions of just plain folks who wanted to enjoy the view.

Presidents

Sixty years after the monument opened to the pubic, Harry S. Truman became the only President to travel to the top of the completed monument. On January 14, 1948, Truman used the vantage point of the monument's observation deck to view locations for a new bridge across the Potomac River. Truman also spoke at the 1948 centennial of the laying of the monument's cornerstone.

Truman was not the first President to be associated with the monument, however. James Madison, fourth President of the United States, was chosen the second president of the Washington National Monument Society in 1835. Madison, who served in the White House from 1809 until 1817, was 85 years old at the time of the appointment.

Because of Madison's advanced age, he treated the role as ceremonial, leaving the management of the society to others. When Madison died in 1836, the society decided to make the sitting President of the United States the ex officio president of the society. Andrew Jackson was the first sitting president to hold the office.

When the cornerstone of the monument was laid in 1848, President James K. Polk attended, despite poor health. Also present were the future 15th, 16th and 17th presidents, James Buchanan, Abraham Lincoln and Andrew Johnson.

A visit to the monument exactly two years later may have caused the death of another President, Zachary Taylor. On July 4, 1850, Taylor sat for several hours in the hot sun during an Independence Day ceremony on the monument grounds. Later in the day, back at the White House, Taylor complained of illness. He died five days later. One report said the illness was brought on by the over consumption of ice cream and cherries.

President Ulysses S. Grant was the monument's patron in the years following the Civil War. The monument had been virtually abandoned for 20 years, and the unfinished stump was a blight on the Washington landscape. Despite critics' calls to tear the structure down, Grant believed the monument should be completed. In 1876 he persuaded Congress to take control of the project and hand it over to the U.S. Army Corps of Engineers.

Grant's successor, Rutherford B. Hayes, presided at the laying of a second cornerstone on August 7, 1880, as the Corps of Engineers prepared to resume construction on the shaft. President and Mrs. Hayes and other dignitaries were hoisted to the top of the unfinished obelisk for the ceremony. Hayes thus became the first president to ride the elevator to the top of the monument, as high as that was at the time —150 feet.

Chester A. Arthur was President when the monument was dedicated on February 21, 1885. Speaking at the event, Arthur said "as President of the United States and in behalf of the people of the United States, I receive this monument from the hands of its builder and declare it dedicated to the immortal name and memory of George Washington."

Arthur's term as President was less than illustrious. He was nominated for the Vice Presidency as a compromise candidate in 1880, on the Republican ticket with James Garfield. When Garfield died from an assassin's bullet in September, 1881, after only six months in office, Arthur ascended to the Presidency. Three years later, he was passed over by his own party for the Presidential nomination. However, of all the Presidents associated with the monument, Arthur's name is the only one inscribed on the aluminum pyramid at the monument's highest point.

In 1946, President Harry S. Truman (center) became the first President to visit the top of the Washington Monument since its completion. He used the monument's observation deck to scout sites for a new bridge across the Potomac River.

The Monument is No Place for a Wedding

In 1950, a young couple was disappointed when the superintendent of the monument refused their request to be married in the monument. National Guardsman Harry Hunt and his fiancée Betty Hansborough, were told that "the Washington Monument is not a church." The superintendent told them he did not want to set a precedent and open the door to a flood of similar requests. Instead the couple was married in a real church.

Hunt and Hansborough should not have been surprised by the decision, however. Friends of theirs had earlier been refused the same request.

No Magic in the Monument

In 1940, the famous magician, Harry Blackstone, saw the Washington Monument as a challenging place to stage a famous illusion. Blackstone wanted to perform his "vanishing horse trick" at the top of the monument.

The *Washington Times-Herald* reported that Blackstone was thwarted in his effort, however, when a guard at the monument refused to let him and his horse board the elevator.

Blackstone said the next time he came to the monument, he would bring an eagle instead of a horse. Then let them try and stop me, the magician said.

Who's on First?
Make That Who's the 27,000,000th?

The anticipated arrival of the 27 millionth visitor to the Washington Monument on June 13, 1953, spurred a publicity stunt that misfired.

Actress Barbara Ashley was in Washington for a performance of the musical "Show Boat." When her publicity agent heard that the monument expected to host its 27 millionth visitor that day, the agent arranged for Ashley to be that visitor.

As the counter on the monument's turnstile clicked nearer to the 27-million mark, Ashley and her agent stood by, waiting for the right moment. Charles Staples, an engineer on the Panama Canal, was visitor 26,999,999. Ashley stepped into the line behind him, and in front of his 15-year-old daughter, Diane.

However, during interviews with the press, both women claimed to be the 27 millionth visitor. Diane, who had not been included in the plan to make the actress the honored guest, had slipped her dime into the turnstile before Ashley stepped into the line, and claimed the distinction for herself. (At the time, the monument charged 10 cents to ride the elevator.)

Not wanting to create an embarrassing scene for either the famous actress or the young woman from the Canal Zone, reporters included both of them in their coverage of the event.

You're Young, You're Pretty, You Win!

Up through the 1960s, the Washington Monument created headlines when it reached another million-visitor mark.

A review of the newspaper articles documenting these milestones turned up a curious coincidence. The distinction was often won by a young, pretty girl. Others to earn the honor have included a young couple on their honeymoon and a mother with a cute baby. It would appear that being photogenic may have been a requirement for being recognized as a millionth visitor.

Congress' original concept for a monument to George Washington was a statue of the general mounted on a horse. When progress on the Washington Monument stalled in the 1850s, Congress resurrected the equestrian statue. It was dedicated in 1860 and stands in Washington Circle, seven blocks from the White House.

Chapter 8

Monumental Cousins

Though perhaps the most famous monument to George Washington, the Washington Monument in Washington, D.C., is not the only monument to our first president. It wasn't even the first.

Nor is the Washington Monument the only building of its kind. This chapter looks at some of the monument's more significant cousins.

George the First: Washington County, Maryland

Twenty-one years before construction began on the monument in our Nation's Capital, the people of Boonsboro in Western Maryland erected their own monument to the First President.

The crude, circular tower of stone stands on South Mountain, in an area young Washington surveyed for Lord Fairfax, and near the route Washington took in 1754 and 1755 en route to his military encounters with the French in Western Pennsylvania.

On July 4, 1827, the people of Boonsboro decided to honor George Washington on Independence Day by building a stone monument in his honor. That morning, the people of the town climbed to Blue Rocks Summit on nearby South Mountain and began their work.

They piled native stones on top of each other until mid-day, when they paused for a picnic and Independence Day speeches. Then they went back to work.

By the end of the day, they had built a tower 30 feet high and 54 feet across, with a stairway leading to its top. Veterans of the Revolutionary War climbed to the top to fire a musket volley. The day's work done, everyone went home.

The crude tower has been rebuilt many times. During the Civil War it was used as a signal post and was damaged by cannon fire.

In 1934, the tower and the land around it were deeded to the state and became what is now Washington Monument State Park. The

Civilian Conservation Corps rebuilt the tower and the monument was rededicated July 4, 1936.

Just for Practice: Baltimore

When Robert Mills submitted his proposal to the Washington National Monument Society, he had already designed one Washington Monument. Mills first design stands in Mount Vernon Square in central Baltimore.

Erected in 1829, the monument stands 178 feet tall.

Like's its cousin in the District of Columbia, Baltimore's monument to Washington also features an interior staircase (228 steps) and an observation area at the top provides a panoramic view of Baltimore.

The Hometown Mason: Alexandria, Va.

Just down the Potomac River and within plain sight of the capital's Washington Monument is the George Washington Masonic Memorial. Standing 333 feet tall on a hill overlooking Alexandria, Va., the monument was built by the Masonic Order to honor one of their own. (Washington was a Mason from age 20 until his death. At one time he held the rank of First Worshipful Master of the Alexandria lodge.)

Designed to resemble the ancient lighthouse at Alexandria, Egypt, the Masonic memorial is a combination George Washington memorial and a monument to Masonic rites and traditions. Unlike its cousin on the Mall, Alexandria's memorial displays artwork and artifacts from Washington's life and times.

Like its more famous cousin, the Masonic memorial has an observation deck with stunning views of Alexandria, Arlington, Va., Washington, D.C., and the Potomac River.

Richmond, Va.: The Face Is Familiar, But...

A statue reputed to be the closest likeness of George Washington in existence stands in the Virginia state capitol in Richmond. Commissioned by the Virginia General Assembly shortly after the end of

J. BERARD

The people of Boonsboro, Md. built this tower on July 4, 1827 to honor the First President. It has been rebuilt several times since then, most recently in 1936.

Jean-Antoine Houdon's statue of George Washington stands in the Virginia state capitol in Richmond. A copy stands in the elevator lobby of the Washington Monument. Some observers think the sculptor made one of Washington's legs longer than the other, but Houdon's defenders say no.

the American Revolution, the statue was carved by the renowned French sculptor Jean-Antoine Houdon. Copies of the Houdon work stand in the elevator lobby of the Washington Monument and in the rotunda of the U.S. Capitol.

In preparation for the sculpture, Houdon spent two weeks as Washington's guest at Mount Vernon in 1785, making plaster casts of Washington's face and body and making detailed measurements of his subject. (Martha Washington's six-year-old granddaughter, Nellie Custis, walked in on Houdon as he was applying plaster to Washington, who was covered in a sheet. The girl became distraught because she thought the General had died.)

Sherwin McRae, author of the official history of the statue by commission of the Virginia legislature, wrote that many distinguished persons who knew Washington personally judged Houdon's work a most accurate likeness. These included Thomas Jefferson, Benjamin Franklin, the Marquis de Lafayette, and Gilbert Stuart, whose portraits of Washington present the likenesses most familiar to the world. Even Horatio Greenough used Houdon's castings for the head and face of his controversial Olympian statue of Washington.

The statue shows Washington, standing erect, dressed in his Revolutionary uniform, holding a sword in one hand and a cane in the other, to represent the balance between military power and civil authority. Fasces and a plow stand at his side, to represent Washington's service in the government and his life as a private citizen.

While Houdon's work is renowned for its close resemblance to its subject, the praise for the likeness is generally reserved for the statue's head and face. Lafayette, for example, made his comments while looking at a bust made from castings of the statue.

However, according to some accounts, the body of the statue is not Washington's at all, but that of Gouverneur Morris of Pennsylvania, one of the signers of the Constitution, then serving as an American diplomat in Paris. Morris posed for Houdon wearing Washington's uniform and boots. Morris was of slightly smaller stature than Washington, and had an artificial leg, which, when shod with Washington's boot, made one leg shorter than the other.

Defenders of Houdon's work dispute this view. Nowhere is this defense more passionate than in Richmond, where Houdon's original stands. The Capitol Hostesses, who provide tours and assist visitors to Virginia's Capitol building, concede that Morris did don Washington's uniform and pose for Houdon, but they contend that the sculptor based the statue's dimensions on the precise measurements he made of Washington's body during his visit to Mount Vernon. The body is Washington's, they insist, not Morris'.

So, it is up to the eye of the beholder to determine if the statue is a true depiction of George Washington, or the head of a President on the body of a Gouverneur.

Vocabulary Lesson:
What the heck are fasces?

Fasces are a bundle of rods tied around an ax, to symbolize strength in the union of equals, the very nature of democracy. The ancient Roman republic first used fasces as a symbol of authority. When the United States chose a democratic government over the rule of the British monarchy, the young country looked to the ancient democracies of Greece and Rome as its historic predecessors and adopted many of their features. It took the term Senate, for example, from the Romans. It also adopted the symbol of the fasces.

In the years leading up to World War II, the symbol was adopted, and corrupted, by Benito Mussolini and the Fascist Party of Italy, whose policies were anything but democratic. Despite Mussolini's use of the symbol, fasces still represent strength through unity to the U. S. Congress. The official seal of the Senate includes fasces, and the symbol decorates the chamber of the House of Representatives.

An Obelisk Ahead: Charlestown, Mass.

In 1827, a group of patriotic citizens in the Boston area formed the Bunker Hill Monument Association to create a monument to the colonists who fought in the first great battle of the American Revolution. The Battle of Bunker Hill was fought in Charlestown, Mass., just across the Charles River from Boston. On June 17, 1775, two months

THIS IS NOT THE WASHINGTON MONUMENT!
*This photograph has been published in books and newspapers
and identified as workmen putting the finishing touches
on the Washington Monument. However these men are actually
working on the Sergeant Floyd Monument at Sioux City,
Iowa. Floyd was a member of the Lewis and Clark expedition
who died on a bluff overlooking the Missouri River in 1804.
The Floyd monument, like the Washington Monument, is
a stone obelisk, but at 100 feet, it is less than one-fifth the height of
its Washington cousin. Construction on the Iowa obelisk began
in 1900, 15 years after completion of the Washington Monument.
Work was completed in 1901. Because this photo is often
misidentified, the Library of Congress maintains a copy in the
file with Washington Monument photographs, but has
emblazoned the copy with the warning,*
"THIS IS NOT THE WASHINGTON MONUMENT."

after the "shot heard round the world" was fired at Concord Bridge, a force of American colonists, estimated from 2,500 to 4,000 strong, held off two attacks by 2,200 experienced British troops. According to legend, the American defenders were told by their commanders to hold their fire, "until you see the whites of their eyes."

The third British attack broke the American lines and chased the colonials off the hill. The British had won the battle, but at a heavy cost. The British casualty rate was nearly 50 percent. The Americans, though defeated, showed they could stand their ground and fight against the greatest army in the world.

The battle was actually fought on Breed's Hill. There are several explanations for the misleading name. One theory is that Colonel William Prescott, commander of the colonial troops, changed strategy at the last minute and fortified the lower but better positioned Breed's Hill instead of the commanding Bunker Hill. Troops from outside the area who were unfamiliar with the local geography were told they were going to fight on Bunker Hill, and that's where they thought they were. A less flattering theory is that the colonial troops who began to fortify the hill the night before the battle simply got lost in the dark of night and fortified the wrong hill.

The society adopted a design by Loammi Baldwin, an obelisk 221 feet tall. The Bunker Hill Monument was dedicated in 1843, five years before construction began on the Washington obelisk.

San Jacinto: Everything's Bigger in Texas

Visitors to the San Jacinto Battleground state park southeast of Houston, Tex. are greeted by a stone tower resembling the Washington Monument, only with a large, five-point star on top.

This is the San Jacinto Monument, built in 1939 to commemorate the decisive 1836 victory by General Sam Houston over the Mexican president and dictator, General Antonio Lopez de Santa Anna, and the establishment of Texas as an independent republic.

The square shaft rises 570 feet above the Texas prairie, making the San Jacinto Monument 15 feet taller than the Washington Monument. However, since the Texas tower is built with steel-reinforced concrete, the Washington Monument still holds the title of the world's tallest free-standing all-masonry structure.

Tall Texan

When the State of Texas built the monument to comemorate the centennial of the 1836 Battle of San Jacinto, it made sure its obelisk stood taller than the Washington Monument. At 570 feet, the San Jacinto Monument, built between 1936 and 1939 southeast of Houston, is 15 feet taller than the Washington Monument.

George Washington as painted by Gilbert Stuart.

Appendix I:
A Short Biography of George Washington

George Washington was born on February 17, 1731. A calendar correction during Washington's lifetime changed the date to February 22, 1732, the date we observe today as Washington's birthday. His parents were Augustine and Mary Washington.

He was born at Wakefield Plantation in Westmoreland County, near present-day Fredericksburg, Va. Part of the plantation is preserved by the National Park Service as Washington's Birthplace National Historic Site.

Washington's father died when George was 11 years old. Two years later, he moved to Mount Vernon, a plantation owned by his brother, Lawrence, along the Potomac River south of Alexandria, Va. As a young man, Washington studied mathematics and was trained as a surveyor.

When Lawrence Washington died in 1752, George, then 20 years old, inherited the estate. The holdings included Mount Vernon plantation and land in other parts of Virginia. In all, Washington inherited 110,000 acres, nearly 172 square miles of land.

Despite his vast land holdings, Washington did not want to be a farmer. His ambition in life was a career in the military, in service to the King as an officer in the regular British army. He began his military career as an officer in the Virginia Militia in 1753.

Washington got his taste of military life in 1754, when the French and Indian War broke out. When British General Edward Braddock died in the battle of Braddock's Field in 1755, Washington lost his hope for a commission in the regular army.

In 1759, Washington married Martha Dandridge Custis, a widow with two children from her previous marriage. After the war, Washington returned to his plantation, and resigned himself to the life of a gentleman farmer. He also served in the Virginia House of Burgesses, the colonial legislature. Washington soon found himself drawn into the growing conflict between Great Britain and her American colonies.

The French and Indian War left Britain with a great debt, and the new territories of Canada and Ohio needed soldiers to defend them. To pay these costs, the British crown imposed taxes on the American colonists. These taxes created an unrest in the colonies that led to the beginnings of the American Revolution.

In June, 1775, the Continental Congress appointed Washington Commander-in-Chief of the colonial forces in their war for independence from Great Britain. His finest hours came in his Christmas crossing of the Delaware River to surprise the Hessian mercenaries at Trenton, N.J., in 1776, and in the defeat of Lord Cornwallis at Yorktown, Va., in 1781, the decisive victory of the war.

Washington's political leadership was called upon in 1787, as the colonies met to devise the new Constitution. Washington was elected to preside over the convention. When it was over and the 13 states ratified the Constitution, Washington was elected the first President of the United States under the new government.

Washington served two terms as President, from 1789 to 1797. He then retired to his beloved Mount Vernon, where he died December 14, 1799.

The Very Model of a Modern President

George Washington was more than simply the first U.S. President. He was the very personification of the office.

When the Framers met in Philadelphia during the summer of 1787 and began debating the shape and form of the new American government, they had to decide on the roles and powers given to each branch of that government.

As the convention debated the duties and responsibilities to be given the President under the new Constitution, it needed only to look to the front of the convention hall, where General Washington, the leader of the Continental Army during the American Revolution, presided over the gathering. Washington's stature as a leader made him the logical choice to be the first President, so the delegates were, in effect, debating what powers and duties should be bestowed upon Washington.

In that way, Washington personified the office of President for many of the men who crafted the Constitution. Later, Washington's term in office set many precedents, both formal and informal, for those who followed.

Washington was such a popular choice for President that he was elected to the office by a unanimous vote of the Electoral College. That feat was to be repeated only once, when Washington unanimously won a second term four years later.

A triangulation party from the U.S. Coast and Geodetic Survey took advantage of scaffolding erected to clean and repair the Washington Monument and climbed to the top of the monument on November 19, 1934 to plot the tower's exact height and location. Sixty-five years later, another Geodectic Survey team scaled the monument again to perform the same measurements using the latest technology. The resulting measurements showed the monument to be at the same location plotted in 1934, but the structure was about three-quarters of an inch taller than calculated by the 1934 survey.

Appendix II:
The Tale of the Tape: Monument Facts & Figures

Height: 555 ft., 5.9 in.

Width (at base): 55 ft. 1.5 in.

Width (at top of shaft): 34 ft., 5.5 in.

Thickness of walls (at base): 15 ft.

Thickness of walls (at top of shaft): 18 in.

Thickness of walls (in pyramid): 7 in.

Depth of foundation: 36 ft.

Weight of monument: 90,854 tons

Sway of monument (in 30 mph wind): 0.125 in.

Original cost of construction: $1,187,710

Number of steps: 897*

Number of blocks used in construction: 36,000

Number of memorial stones: 194

---

*The monument staircase originally had 898 steps,
but one was eliminated in 1976 when it was replaced
with a ramp to make the monument more accessible
for handicapped visitors.*

The Incredible Growing Monument

During the 1999 renovations, scientists and technicians from the National Geodetic Survey used sophisticated instruments to measure the Washington Monument's size and location.

The survey determined that the building actually stands 555 ft., 5.9 in. tall, more than 3/4 in. taller than earlier measurements had indicated.

Does this mean the monument is growing? No, said the survey team. The team attributed the difference in numbers to the use of modern, more accurate instruments.

The survey also found that, although the monument appeared to have grown, it hadn't moved. The monument is at the same longitude and latitude it was when the Geodetic Survey last calculated its position in 1934.

Taller vs. Higher

The Washington Monument is the tallest building in Washington, D.C., but it is not the highest. That distinction belongs to the Washington National Cathedral.

The cathedral's main tower stands 301 ft. above the ground, considerably shorter than the monument's 555-ft. height. However, the cathedral stands on one of the highest points in the city. When measured against sea level, the cathedral reaches 676 ft. into the sky, while the monument only reaches 596 ft. above sea level.

Therefore, of the two buildings, the Washington Monument is taller, but the National Cathedral is higher.

How Does the Washington Monument Stack Up?

The monument's height compared with other tall buildings of the world:

CN Tower, Toronto	1,821 ft.
Taipei 101, Taipei	1,670 ft.
Sears Tower, Chicago	1,450 ft.
World Trade Center, New York	*1,368 ft.*
Empire State Building, New York	1,250 ft.
Eiffel Tower, Paris	984 ft.
Gateway Arch, St. Louis	630 ft.
Washington Monument	**555 ft.**
Great Pyramid, Giza, Egypt	451 ft.
Statue of Liberty, New York	305 ft.
National Cathedral, Washington	301 ft.
U.S. Capitol, Washington	287 ft.
Leaning Tower, Pisa	191 ft.

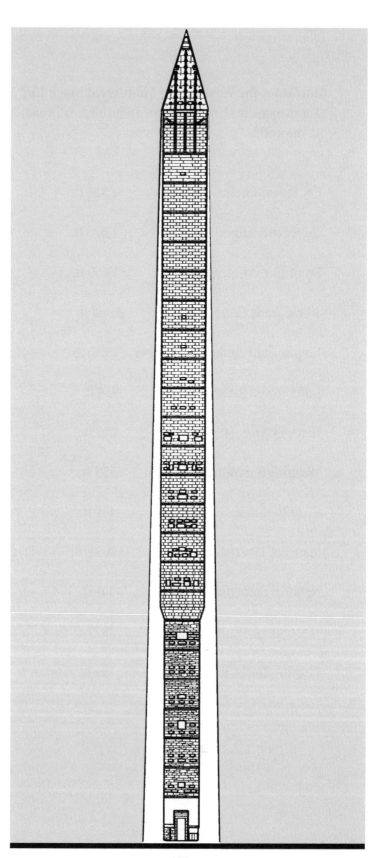

130

Appendix III:
Inventory of Memorial Stones

30 feet
George Watterston, Secretary of the
  Washington National Monument Society
National Greys of Washington, D.C.
Franklin Fire Co., Washington, D.C.
Little Falls Quarry, District of Columbia
State of Delaware
State of Maine
State of Arkansas

40 feet
Columbia Typographical Society
Association of Journeymen Stone Cutters of Philadelphia
German Benevolent Society, Washington, D.C.
State of Alabama
State of Louisiana
City of Nashville, Tenn.

50 feet
Washington Light Infantry, Washington, D.C.
Grand Lodge (Masons), Washington, D.C.
State of Illinois
Washington Naval Lodge No. 4 (Masons),
  Washington, D.C.
State of Georgia
State of Indiana

60 feet
Anacostia Tribe, Improved Order of Red Men,
  Washington, D.C.
Grand Lodge (Odd Fellows), New Jersey
Westmoreland County, Va.
State of Florida
State of New Hampshire
State of South Carolina

[Between 60 ft. and 70 ft. levels is a stone marking the point 100 ft. from bottom of foundation]

70 feet
Grand Division (Sons of Temperance), Virginia
United Sons of America, Pennsylvania
Grand Division (Sons of Temperance), North Carolina
State of Connecticut
State of Massachusetts
State of New Jersey

80 feet
Maryland Pilgrims Association
Grand Lodge (Odd Fellows), Indiana
Invincible Fire Co., Cincinnati, Ohio
State of Maryland
City of Washington, D.C.
State of Virginia

90 feet
Mechanics of Raleigh, N.C.
Odd Fellows of Ohio
City of Little Rock, Ark.
State of Mississippi
State of Ohio
State of Missouri

100 feet
Independent Order of United Brothers, Maryland
Citizens of Thomaston, Maine (Home of Knox)
Grand Lodge (Odd Fellows), Virginia
State of Rhode Island
State of North Carolina
State of Wisconsin

110 feet
Grand Lodge (Masons) of Ohio
Grand Lodge (Masons) of Kentucky
Grand Lodge (Masons) of New York
State of Iowa
Postmasters and Assistant Postmasters of Indiana

120 feet

Patmos Lodge No. 20 (Masons), Ellicott Mills, Md.
Odd Fellows lodges of Germantown, Pa.
Sons of Temperance, Rhode Island
City of Roxbury, Mass.
State of California
City of Frederick, Md.
Mount Lebanon Lodge (Masons), Lebanon, Pa.
City of Durham, N.H.
Washington Lodge No. 21 (Masons), New York, N.Y.
Grand Lodge (Masons) of Maryland
Oakland College, Mississippi
City of New York
Alumni of Washington College, Lexington, Va.
Grand Division (Sons of Temperance), Connecticut
Union Society, Hillsborough, N.C.
American Institute, New York, N.Y.
American Whig Society, Princeton, N.J.
Odd Fellows, Massachusetts

140 feet

Engineers, James River and Kanaweh Canal
Company I, 4th Regiment, Infantry, U.S. Army
Otter's Summit, Virginia
Fort Greene Guard, Brooklyn, N.Y.
Grand Lodge (Masons) of Illinois
Masterton and Smith, Westchester County, N.Y.
Grand Lodge (Masons) of Georgia
City of Baltimore, Md.
Grand Lodge (Masons) of Alabama
Hittner's Quarry, Montgomery County, Pa.

150 feet

[There are no memorial stones at this level]

160 feet

State of New York
Eureka Lodge (Odd Fellows), New York
City of Newark, N.J.
Athenian Lodge (Odd Fellows), Troy, N.Y.

City of Warren, R.I.
Lafayette Lodge (Masons), New York, N.Y.

170 feet
State of Vermont
City of Boston, Mass.
City of Salem, Mass.
City of New Bedford, Mass.
City of Charlestown, Mass.
Washington Lodge (Masons), Roxbury, Mass.

180 feet
State of Pennsylvania
City of Philadelphia, Pa.
Grand Lodge (Masons) of Pennsylvania
Sons of Temperance, Pennsylvania
Odd Fellows, Pennsylvania

190 feet
Brazil
Siam (Thailand)
Bremen, Germany
Free Swiss Confederation (Switzerland)
Ottoman Empire (Turkey)
Greece
Greek Islands of Paros and Naxos

200 feet
State of West Virginia
City of Richmond, Va.
Templars of Honor and Temperance
Grand Lodge (Masons) of Virginia
Grand Lodge (Odd Fellows) of Maryland
Grand Lodge (Odd Fellows) of the United States
St. John's Lodge (Masons), Richmond, Va.

210 feet
State of Kansas
State of Michigan
Grand Lodge (Masons) of Iowa

Independent Order of Odd Fellows, U.S.A.
Grand Division (Sons of Temperance) of Ohio
Grand Lodge (Odd Fellows) of Mississippi
Grand Lodge (Masons) of Arkansas
Grand Division (Sons of Temperance), Illinois

220 feet

State of Montana
State of Oregon
State of Minnesota
Japan
Christians in China
State of Wyoming
Cherokee Nation
State of Nebraska
State of Utah/Territory of Deseret
State of Nevada

230 feet

Grand Lodge (Odd Fellows) of Kentucky
State of Kentucky
Georgia Convention
Hawkins County, Tenn.
Grand Lodge (Masons) of Florida
State of Tennessee

240 feet

American Medical Association
Presbyterian Church in the U.S.A.
Tuscarora Tribe No. 5, Improved Order of Red Men,
    Washington, D.C.
Kings County, N.Y.
Wales
Oldest Inhabitants of the District of Columbia
United American Mechanics, Pennsylvania
From Braddock's Field (Pennsylvania)

250 feet

Thalian Association of Wilmington, N.C.
Philadelphia Fire Dept. (3 stones)

Citizens of U.S. residing in Foo Chow Foo, China
Citizens of Stockton, Ca.
Proprietors of the *Cincinnati Commercial*
Ladies of Lowell, Mass.
Teachers of the Buffalo Public Schools
Young Men's Mercantile Library Association of Cincinnati

260 feet
Methodist Episcopal Church, New York, N.Y.
Fire Department, City of New York
Sabbath School Children, Methodist Episcopal Church,
    Philadelphia
Washington Erina Guard, Newark, N.J.
Pupils of the Public Schools, Baltimore, Md.
Cincinnati Company
Sons of New England in Canada

270 feet
Cleosophic Society, Nassau Hall, N.J.
Continental Guard, New Orleans, La.
R. Norris and Sons Locomotive Works, Philadelphia, Pa.
Ladies of Manchester, N.H. (Home of Stark)
Alexandria Library in Egypt, from G.G. Baker
Jefferson Society, University of Virginia

280 feet
Western Military Institute, Drennon, Ky.
Honesdale, Wayne County, Pa.
First Regiment of Light Infantry, Boston, Mass.
Two Disciples of Daguerre
Hibernian Society of Baltimore, Md.
City of Alexandria, Va.
Jefferson Medical College of Philadelphia, Pa.
Dramatic Profession of America

290 ft.
State of Oklahoma
State of Colorado
State of Texas

300 ft.
State of South Dakota

310 ft.
State of Washington
Okinawa Prefecture, Japan

320 ft.
State of Arizona

330 feet
State of New Mexico
Stone marking elevation of top of U.S. Capitol

340 ft.
Pope's Stone replacement (Donated by
　Father James Grant)

350 ft.
State of North Dakota

360 ft.
State of Hawaii

380 ft.
Carthage Stone donated by David Heap

400 ft.
State of Idaho

450 ft.
State of Alaska

Sources and Bibliography

Bibliography

Clark, Harrison. *All Cloudless Glory*. 2 vols.
    Washington: Regnery Publishing, Inc., 1996.

Cunliffe, Marcus. *George Washington, Man and
    Monument*. New York: Mentor Books, 1958.

Doherty, Craig A. and Katherine M. *The Washington
    Monument*. Woodbridge, Conn.:
    Blackbirch Press, 1995.

Freidel, Frank and Aikman, Lonelle. *George
    Washington, Man and Monument*. 3rd ed.
    Washington: National Geographic, 1988.

Irving, Washington. *George Washington,
    A Biography*. New York: Da Capo Press, 1976.

McRae, Sherwin. *The Houdon Statue, Its History
    and Value*. Richmond: Superintendent of Public
    Printing, 1873.

Torres, Louis. *"To the Immortal Name and Memory
    of George Washington"*. Washington:
    Government Printing Office, 1985.

Washington, George. *Last Will and Testament*.
    Washington, D.C.: A. Jackson, 1868.

Other Sources

Arnold, David
Baltimore Sun
Capitol Hostesses, Richmond, Va.
Gallaudet University
Grant, Father James
Guinness Book of World Records
Historical Society of Washington
Library of Congress
Maryland Department of Natural Resources
National Archives and Records Administration
National Park Service, U.S. Department of the Interior
National Geodetic Survey, National Oceanic
    and Atmospheric Administration
Parade
Ripley's Believe It or Not!
Smithsonian Institution
Smithsonian Magazine
Texas Parks and Wildlife Department
U.S. Army Corps of Engineers
U.S.S. Constitution Museum
Utah State Historical Society
Vaughn, Carol
Washington Times
Washington Times-Herald
Washington Daily News
Washington Star
Washington Post
Washingtoniana Division, D.C. Public Library
Wood, Phil, WTEM Radio
World Almanac and Book of Facts

*The author standing next to a scale model of the Washington
Monument and in front of the real thing in 1999. Note Michael
Graves' mesh cover on the scaffolding, designed to mimic
the pattern of the Monument's marble blocks durng
the 1998-2000 renovations.*

About the Author

JIM BERARD served as a volunteer at the Washington Monument from 1993 to 1999 under the National Park Service's Volunteers in the Parks program, providing visitor information and conducting walk-down tours of the monument's stairway.

A Capitol Hill press secretary since 1987, Berard is the Communications Director for the House Committee on Transportation and Infrastructure. Prior to coming to Washington, Berard spent 15 years as a journalist for radio stations and newspapers in Iowa, Minnesota and his home state of Illinois. His broadcasting career included six state and regional awards for news and editorial writing as News Director at KWEB-KRCH radio in Rochester, Minn., and five years as the producer of "Common Ground," a nationally syndicated radio documentary series on international affairs produced by the Stanley Foundation of Muscatine, Iowa.

Berard has a degree in Speech Communications from Northern Illinois University (1978) and has done graduate study in journalism at the University of Iowa, and non-credit course work at the U.S. Department of Agriculture Graduate School in Washington.

He is also the author of *The Capitol Inside and Out* (2003).

Volunteer Opportunities
With the National Park Service

Each year more than 130,000 Americans volunteer their time and abilities to help operate and maintain national parks, monuments, historic sites and other properties managed by the National Park Service.

Volunteers come from all walks of life and every age group. They perform a variety of duties, from staffing information desks and kiosks to leading tours and educational programs, and building and maintaining trails, buildings and other park facilities.

Information on volunteer opportunities and applications for volunteer positions are available at each National Park Service unit.

Library of Congress Photo Reference Information

Page 10	Original Design of Washington Monument	LC-USZ62-51521
Page 15	Subscription Certificate	LC-USZ62-2773
Page 18	Early Construction	LC-USZ62-5728
Page 24	1891 Drawings	LC-USZ62-24667
Page 31	Floodlight, 1923	LC-USZ62-59532
Page 42	Baseball Card, 1911-Front 1912-Back	Lot 13163-29, no. 89 Lot 13163-30, no. 168
Page 49	Army Blimp	LC-USZ62-91908
Page 83	In the Elevator	LC-USZ62-59907
Page 85	Stairway Landing	HABS DC, WASH, 2-102
Page 89	Cutaway View of Stairway	HABS-DC-426
Page 111	Houdon Statue *(Virginia Chamber of Commerce Photo by Flournoy)*	LC-USZ62-7886
Page 119	Sgt. Floyd Monument	LC-USZ62-8094
Page 122	Washington Portrait	LC-USZ62-7588
Page 130	Cutaway View of Interior	HABS-DC-426

National Archives Photo Reference Information

All National Archives graphic material in this book came from Record Group 42, with the exception of the photo of President Truman on page 109, which was provided by the Harry S. Truman Presidential Library in Independence, Mo., reference number NLT-AVC-PHT-73 (2139).